Buried Words

THE AZRIELI SERIES OF HOLOCAUST SURVIVOR MEMOIRS: PUBLISHED TITLES

Buried Words: The Diary of Molly Applebaum

Molly Applebaum

THE AZRIELI FOUNDATION
www.azrielifoundation.org

Cover and book design by Mark Goldstein
Endpaper maps by Martin Gilbert
Map on page xxxi by François Blanc
Translation of Molly Applebaum's diary by Textura Foundation, Poland, 2014.
Editing and notations in Molly's diary by Professor Jan Grabowski, University of Ottawa, 2017.

LIBRARY AND ARCHIVES CANADA CATALOGUING IN PUBLICATION

Applebaum, Molly, 1930–
[Diaries. Selections]
    Buried words: the diary of Molly Applebaum / Molly Applebaum.

Includes index.
ISBN 978-1-988065-12-0 (softcover)

1. Applebaum, Molly, 1930– — Diaries. 2. Jews — Persecutions — Poland — Dąbrowa Tarnowska — Diaries. 3. Holocaust, Jewish (1939–1945) — Poland — Dąbrowa Tarnowska — Personal narratives. 4. Hiding places — Poland — Dąbrowa Tarnowska. I. Azrieli Foundation, issuing body II. Title.

DS134.72.A67A3 2017   940.53'18092   C2017-901925-2

PRINTED IN CANADA

The Azrieli Series of Holocaust Survivor Memoirs

Naomi Azrieli, Publisher

Jody Spiegel, Program Director
Arielle Berger, Managing Editor
Farla Klaiman, Editor
Matt Carrington, Editor
Elizabeth Lasserre, Senior Editor, French-Language Editions
Elin Beaumont, Senior Education Outreach and Program Facilitator
Catherine Person, Educational Outreach and Events Coordinator,
    Quebec and French Canada
Marc-Olivier Cloutier, Educational Outreach and Events Assistant,
    Quebec and French Canada
Tim MacKay, Digital Platform Manager
Elizabeth Banks, Digital Asset Curator and Archivist
Susan Roitman, Office Manager (Toronto)
Mary Mellas, Executive Assistant and Human Resources (Montreal)

Mark Goldstein, Art Director
François Blanc, Cartographer
Bruno Paradis, Layout, French-Language Editions

Contents

Series Preface:
In their own words. . .

In telling these stories, the writers have liberated themselves. For so many years we did not speak about it, even when we became free people living in a free society. Now, when at last we are writing about what happened to us in this dark period of history, knowing that our stories will be read and live on, it is possible for us to feel truly free. These unique historical documents put a face on what was lost, and allow readers to grasp the enormity of what happened to six million Jews — one story at a time.

David J. Azrieli, C.M., C.Q., M.Arch
Holocaust survivor and founder, The Azrieli Foundation

Since the end of World War II, over 30,000 Jewish Holocaust survivors have immigrated to Canada. Who they are, where they came from, what they experienced and how they built new lives for themselves and their families are important parts of our Canadian heritage. The Azrieli Foundation's Holocaust Survivor Memoirs Program was established to preserve and share the memoirs written by those who survived the twentieth-century Nazi genocide of the Jews of Europe and later made their way to Canada. The program is guided by the conviction that each survivor of the Holocaust has a remarkable story to tell, and that such stories play an important role in education about tolerance and diversity.

Millions of individual stories are lost to us forever. By preserving the stories written by survivors and making them widely available to a broad audience, the Azrieli Foundation's Holocaust Survivor Memoirs Program seeks to sustain the memory of all those who perished at the hands of hatred, abetted by indifference and apathy. The personal accounts of those who survived against all odds are as different as the people who wrote them, but all demonstrate the courage, strength, wit and luck that it took to prevail and survive in such terrible adversity. The memoirs are also moving tributes to people — strangers and friends — who risked their lives to help others, and who, through acts of kindness and decency in the darkest of moments, frequently helped the persecuted maintain faith in humanity and courage to endure. These accounts offer inspiration to all, as does the survivors' desire to share their experiences so that new generations can learn from them.

The Holocaust Survivor Memoirs Program collects, archives and publishes these distinctive records and the print editions are available free of charge to educational institutions and Holocaust-education programs across Canada. They are also available for sale to the general public at bookstores. All revenues to the Azrieli Foundation from the sales of the Azrieli Series of Holocaust Survivor Memoirs go toward the publishing and educational work of the memoirs program.

~

The Azrieli Foundation would like to express appreciation to the following people for their invaluable efforts in producing this book: Doris Bergen, Sherry Dodson (Maracle Inc), Jerzy Giebułtowski, Jan Grabowski, Barbara Kamieński, Therese Parent, and Margie Wolfe & Emma Rodgers of Second Story Press.

About the Glossary

The following memoir contains a number of terms, concepts and historical references that may be unfamiliar to the reader. For information on major organizations; significant historical events and people; geographical locations; religious and cultural terms; and foreign-language words and expressions that will help give context and background to the events described in the text, please see the glossary beginning on page 119.

Introduction

I became aware of the existence of Molly Applebaum's diary quite by chance, in the fall of 2012, while giving an advanced graduate seminar on the history of the Holocaust at the University of Ottawa. Shortly before the end of the term, Jason, one of my students, casually mentioned that his grandmother had survived the war in Poland as a child and, while in hiding, she had kept a diary. That same day, I received scanned copies of his grandmother's diary. Written in excellent Polish, on pages yellowed with age, the diary was a heart-wrenching read. I was astonished to see that the author of the diary not only had spent two years underground (quite literally, in a box buried under the dirt floor of a barn) but that she had also survived the German occupation in Dąbrowa Tarnowska, a small town that was the subject of my most recent book, *Judenjagd Polowanie na Żydów 1942–1945*, published in Poland the year before and published in English as *Hunt for the Jews: Betrayal and Murder in German-Occupied Poland* (2013).

The testimony of Melania Weissenberg — the author's maiden name — is one of those unique sources that forces us to revise our own understanding of the past and to reflect on human nature. First of all, from a historian's viewpoint, diaries as a form of historical testimony are considered a source of very particular nature and extraordinary value. Unlike memoirs and accounts written after the fact, the diaries (and especially intimate diaries, such as the one written by

Melania) are free of "corrections of memory" that tend to eliminate and obfuscate those dimensions of our experience that we are least proud of or that we would prefer to sidestep and altogether erase. On top of that, very few diaries that were written by children during the Holocaust have survived the war. The diaries of Anne Frank, Mary Berg, Dawidek Rubinowicz, Rutka Laskier, Renia Knoll, or the slightly older Dawid Sierakowiak, given their unique perspective, count among the most rare and most precious testimonies of the time. Melania started to write her diary as a precocious twelve-year-old girl and finished as a fourteen-year-old woman, deeply marked by the Holocaust. The diary, written between 1942 and 1945, spent the next sixty-seven years in a drawer. Molly's children, who did not know Polish, could not recognize the importance of the diary, and the author herself was not eager to share it with others.

Melania Weissenberg was born in Krakow, Poland, in 1930. Her father, Chaskiel, had a small all-purpose store on Kopernika Street, in the centre of the city. In 1938, after he passed away, Melania's mother, Salomea (also called Sara), took over the family business. Shortly before the war, Salomea married Ignac Keller, one of the recent deportees from Nazi Germany. Melania's stepfather was one of the thousands of Jews, Polish citizens, who, in October 1938, had been arrested throughout Germany, placed on trains and cars and dumped at the Polish border. After the wedding, Salomea decided, for business reasons, to keep her old name, Weissenberg. Melania's mother spoke excellent Polish — a rare feat among the largely unassimilated Polish Jews whose mother tongue was most often Yiddish and who spoke Polish with an accent. It was this legacy and this capital that Salomea left to her daughter, and it was to become crucial during the German occupation.

The war brought immediate chaos to Melania, her younger brother, Zygmunt (diminutively called Zyga), and her parents. The Germans entered their native Krakow on September 6, 1939, after less than a week of fighting. Before the end of the year, the Weissenbergs saw dramatic changes in their lives: they lost their business and their apartment and had to move; their social and economic situation deteriorated quickly. There was nothing particular about the Weissenbergs — they simply shared the common, tragic fate of millions of Polish Jews who found themselves under German rule.

The German occupation in Poland brought about a host of anti-Jewish measures, some of which were implemented before the end of 1939. The Polish state had been abolished and in its place the Germans created a rump state called the General Government *(General-gouvernement)* ruled by Hitler's trusted associate, Hans Frank. One of the most "recognizable" German measures was the "branding" regulation, which, starting on December 1, 1939, required all Polish Jews above the age of twelve to wear white armbands with a blue Star of David. The first ghetto was established in October 1939, although the majority of Polish Jews would find themselves in the ghettos somewhat later, in 1940 and in 1941.

Furthermore, the German authorities introduced a variety of measures that severely restricted the mobility of the Jewish population — even before the establishment of the ghettos. Jews were prohibited from using public transportation; sometimes, special tramways or wagons "nur für Juden" (only for Jews) were placed on the city streets. In some cases Jews were allowed to use only a designated part of a sidewalk, and in other areas they were pushed off the sidewalks altogether and — quite literally — forced to walk in the gutters. This was one of the many shaming and humiliating regulations, as was the requirement to take off one's hat and to bow deeply whenever encountering a German on the street.

While shaming and incarcerating the Jews, the Germans also moved against the foundations of Jewish economic well-being: some professions were declared off-limits for Jews, Jewish retirees lost pensions and Jewish real estate was seized by the authorities. In Krakow this happened earlier than elsewhere: thousands of Jewish businesses (like the Weissenbergs' family business) were taken away from their owners and transferred to the so-called trustees (*Treuhänder*) appointed by the occupier as early as the winter of 1939. In January 1940, the anti-Jewish measures were further reinforced and the German authorities began to seize not only Jewish houses but also their movable property, such as furniture and personal items.

In Krakow, the new capital of occupied Poland, in order to please Governor General Hans Frank who openly expressed his hatred for Jews, the local authorities decided to remove all of them from the city. In May 1940, the 70,000 Jews of Krakow were therefore expelled. It is most likely around that time that Melania and her family decided to flee. Having lost their livelihood and apartment, they sought the help of Sara's sister and other relatives who lived in Dąbrowa Tarnowska, a small town located just over one hundred kilometres east of Krakow, north of Tarnów.

In 1940, when Melania, Zyga, their mother and stepfather arrived in Dąbrowa Tarnowska, the local Jews lived in an open ghetto, without fences or walls separating the "Jewish quarter" from the "Aryan" side. Originally, the Jewish population of the city had numbered 2,500, but with the influx of refugees and deportees, it quickly swelled to 3,500. The Dąbrowa ghetto was located in the eastern part of the city, squeezed into three city blocks.

On January 25, 1940, the Germans appointed Eliezer Weinberger, a local lawyer, to head the Jewish Council (Judenrat), while the Jewish police (Ordnungsdienst; OD), made up of twenty agents, came under the authority of one Kalman Fenichel. While the Judenrat and the OD were created and appointed by the Germans, the Jews of Dąbrowa started to organize their own institutions as well. First and foremost was the Jewish Social Self-Help (Żydowska Samopomoc Społeczna; żss), which was tasked with caring for the poorest members of the ghetto society. Between January and December 1941, the kitchens financed by the Jewish Self-Help fed, on average, four hundred people each day. During the summer and fall of that year, when the hunger in the ghetto reached epidemic proportions, the Judenrat

continued to give out seventy grams of bread daily to the most desti-
tute. To care for the sick, the żss established a small clinic, headed by
Dr. Teufel, himself a deportee from Bielsko. Later on, in the winter of
1941–1942, the Dąbrowa ghetto was separated from the "Aryan" side
of the city, in part by a wooden fence and in part by barbed wire. Despite the new restrictions on movement, leaving the ghetto was not
really much of a problem. The problem was how to survive on the
outside, among Christian neighbours.

With every passing month the situation of the Polish Jews became more and more precarious. On October 15, 1941, the German
authorities in Krakow issued a new law known as the "III Regulation
concerning the Limitations of the Right of Residence in the General-
gouvernement." The most important part of the new law imposed
the death penalty on Jews apprehended outside the ghetto without
authorization. Until then, Jews caught on the "Aryan side" had been
arrested and fined, or sent to prison. Now, it was their lives that were
at stake. The same penalty was imposed on all those who aided and
abetted Jews on the run.

If anyone had doubts as to the Germans' true designs, they were
put to rest in the first days of November 1941, when the German Order Police (orpo-Ordnungspolizei) in Warsaw started to transfer
Jews apprehended outside the ghetto into the custody of the collabo-
rationist Polish "Blue" Police, an especially ruthless and deadly force
that would also become an essential partner of the Germans in the
upcoming execution of the "Final Solution to the Jewish question" in
the Dąbrowa Tarnowska area and elsewhere in occupied Poland. At
the same time, the policemen received instructions to shoot women
and children caught trying to cross from the ghetto to the Aryan side
(similar regulations regarding Jewish men had been issued several
days earlier). Ultimately, on November 17 and December 15, 1941, the
Polish "Blue" Police conducted two mass executions of Jews found
outside the ghetto.

Warsaw was far away from Dąbrowa Tarnowska, but the news

about the executions travelled fast. The executions were made public for a good reason: a part of the German plan was to keep the Jews in a state of constant fear and uncertainty of the future. The threats (sometimes real, sometimes just fearful gossip) contributed to growing panic among the ghetto dwellers. In the early spring of 1942, the Jews of Dąbrowa Tarnowska started to hear more disturbing news about the fate of the Jewish communities in and around Lublin. Starting in March 1942, the Lublin ghetto was progressively liquidated, its population herded into cattle wagons and taken away to a small location called Bełżec. Nothing certain was known about the fate of the "resettled" Jews, but, with time, more horrifying stories started to circulate among the Polish Jews. Unbeknownst to them, Operation Reinhardt, the plan for the total massacre of European Jewry, had begun.

On April 28, 1942, the Jews of Dąbrowa Tarnowska learned firsthand about the new German strategy. On that day the German police from nearby Tarnów and Mielec showed up in the ghetto, armed with lists of wanted people. A few score of prominent local Jews — lawyers, doctors, businessmen and community leaders — were seized, tortured and publicly executed, for all to see. Among the dead was Max Kunstler, Melania's uncle, who was shot by the Germans in front of their house. Melania saw Kunstler's body left for several hours in a pool of blood. Although the local Jews did not know this, the "action" conducted in the Dąbrowa ghetto was part of a larger plan of increased terror and a prelude to mass murder. The plan, conceived by the Krakow Gestapo, targeted the leaders of Jewish communities and was intended to instill fear into the ghetto inhabitants and to take away from the Jews any will to resist before the final liquidation "actions." Similar "actions" took place in other districts of occupied Poland. In the Warsaw ghetto, for instance, during the *Aktion* of April 18, 1942, fifty people, also chosen from a list, were shot in the streets. About that time, the Jews of Dąbrowa started to prepare for the worst, building ingenious hideouts under houses, inside double walls, and in attics. The plan was to survive the initial fury of the Germans, wait until the police were gone and emerge from the hideouts to live another day. The idea that the as-yet not-known-about "Final Solution" was, indeed, final, was not a concept that the Jews of Dąbrowa were ready to accept.

Sometime in the spring of 1942, Melania started to write her diary. In the beginning her thoughts were mostly focused on her friends and family. She wrote about her young love and about her fascination with books. Soon, however, the horrors of everyday life found their way into the pages of the diary.

One month after the executions in the Dąbrowa Tarnowska ghetto, the Germans started to liquidate the large ghetto in Krakow. The main liquidation action started on May 30 and lasted until June 8, 1942. The news about the destruction of Jewish Krakow quickly reached Melania's ghetto, although no one knew anything precise about the fate of the deportees. Some thought (and hoped) that liquidations were similar to previous sweeps that had been organized from time to time by the Germans to send Jews to labour camps.

After the *Aktion* of April 28, 1942, there came a lull. In June, however, several hundred people were taken away to Tarnów, from where they were sent straight to the gas chambers of Bełżec. The main "liquidation action" in Dąbrowa took place on July 17, 1942, when close to two thousand Jews were deported to Bełżec and one hundred others were executed in the streets. Many inhabitants of the Dąbrowa Tarnowska ghetto expected the imminent *Aktion* and went into the hideouts that were usually located inside their houses. One of them was twelve-year-old Melania Weissenberg, who hid in the attic of her own house. She emerged from hiding after the sweep had ended.

After the July liquidation action, when the future existence of the ghetto became highly unlikely and reports about the gas chambers in Bełżec became too numerous to leave any room for doubt, Salomea decided to place her daughter out of harm's way, on the "Aryan" side. Although the ghetto was an open one, survival on the outside was contingent upon good contacts with Poles who would agree to take Jews under their roof. Without Polish assistance the Jews leaving the ghetto stood no chance — and the death penalty introduced by the Germans served as a powerful reminder of risks associated with rescue attempts.

The death penalty was only one of the reasons why Jews found survival on the "Aryan" side so extremely difficult. The Germans had, after all, introduced the death penalty for a number of "crimes" against their rule: Poles faced death for involvement in any kind of resistance, for failing to deliver quotas of livestock or grains, or even for listening to the radio. There was, however, no shortage of volunteers for the resistance, and peasants massively resisted the imposed quotas. There was a broad social consensus and social solidarity in Polish society surrounding these issues. In the case of sheltering Jews, there was no such consensus. Quite to the contrary, those who decided to assist Jews set out on a very lonely journey and exposed themselves to the wrath of many members of their own communities, their neighbours and, not infrequently, their families. Since there was little social approval and acceptance for hiding Jews, the risk of denunciation became the most deadly of all dangers facing the rescuers and their Jewish charges. It was not the Germans, who had little idea of where Jews were hidden, but the hostile attitude of one's neighbours that made aiding the Jewish refugees in occupied Poland quite possibly the most dangerous type of resistance.

It was in the face of these dangers that Salomea Weissenberg approached Wiktor (Victor) Wójcik, a Polish peasant whom she had earlier met at the local market and from whom, from time to time, she had bought produce. Wójcik, together with his widowed sister, Eugenia (Emilia) Kułaga, and her three children, lived on Eugenia's farm close to Dąbrowa Tarnowska. In early September, after a meeting with Salomea, he agreed to take under his roof Melania and Helena, Melania's much older cousin, as well as Salomea and Zyga. They left the ghetto for the farm on September 11, 1942. Ignac joined them about a week later but, finding conditions intolerable, returned to Dąbrowa Tarnowska with Zyga. Ignac and Zyga were later transported to the Tarnów ghetto, sixteen kilometres away. In late October, Zyga escaped a transport and managed to find his way back to the farm, but his eagerness to play and live the life of a typical child, like that of Eugenia's children, put the family at risk. As well, maintaining secrecy and feeding such a large number of people seemed an impossible task. Reluctantly, Wójcik agreed to continue to shelter the girls, but he requested that Salomea and Zyga leave. By the end of December, Salomea had taken Zyga to the Tarnów ghetto. Melania was never to see them again. In leaving Melania and Helena on the farm, Melania's mother was doing what thousands of other Jewish parents were doing at the time — desperately seeking safety for their children.

From unconfirmed stories gathered after the war from Jewish survivors, Melania learned that her mother was later killed in the Tarnów ghetto during one of the liquidation actions. She was unable to learn anything at all about the fate of her younger brother, Zyga, and her stepfather, Ignac.

Wójcik's sister had been informed about the two Jewish girls hidden in the barn, but her children were kept in the dark. The shelter for Melania and Helena was seen as a stopgap measure; the situation, one assumed, would somehow improve, return to normal, and the girls would rejoin their families. No one thought that they would spend the next two and a half years in hiding.

For young Melania the flight from the ghetto meant, above all, separation from her dearest friend, twenty-year-old Sabina Goldman. Sabina, adored and loved by Melania, remained in Dąbrowa Tarnowska and the girls were never to see each other again. Barely one week after Melania's arrival on the farm, the long-expected catastrophe struck the ghetto in Dąbrowa. On September 18, 1942, German and Ukrainian troops, with the help of the Polish "Blue" Police, surrounded the ghetto and started to clear it, house after house. On that day more than eight hundred remaining Jews were loaded onto a death train, and twenty members of the Dąbrowa Jewish Council were shot in the Jewish cemetery.

After this action at least a few hundred Jews remained hidden in the ghetto, sometimes in very elaborate yet discreet hideouts. They were successively discovered and pulled out from their bunkers. Some of them were sent to Bełżec, while others were shot on the spot: "The victims were brought to the cemetery, where they linked their arms and sang Hallel. The German gendarmes threw them on the ground, and officer Bove stood on their bellies and shot them through the mouth," reported one of the survivors.[1] The last remaining Jews — some thirty Jewish policemen and their families — remained locked up in one of the ghetto houses. On December 20, 1942, they, too, were shot at the Jewish cemetery. And that is how the Dąbrowa Tarnowska ghetto ceased to exist.

In January 1943, Wójcik and his sister (referred to by Melania and Helena with certain irony as "our Uncle" and "our Lady"), fearful of nosy neighbours and Eugenia's own children, decided to move the girls to a new, more secure hideout. Thus, Melania and Helena found themselves buried underground, in a large box under the floor of the barn. Once or twice a day the girls were allowed to leave the box in order to wash and to relieve themselves. It was in this box, unable even to sit up, that Melania and Helena were to remain hidden for the next two years, until the arrival of the Soviet army in January 1945. Throughout this time Melania kept her diary close by, although the entries became more and more sparse once the girls were placed underground. The diary (and a small stack of photographs) was all that provided Melania with a link to her previous life.

During the winter, spring and summer of 1943, the diary started

---

1   The archive of the Jewish Historical Institute in Warsaw (AŻIH), collection 301, file 2348, testimony of Alter Milet. *Hallel* comprises Psalms 113 to 118 and is recited on various Jewish holidays in praise of God.

to reflect Melania's overwhelming fear, but it also bore witness to her constant hunger and thirst. The "Uncle," afraid of ever-watchful neighbours (after all, if one were to draw more buckets from the well, it could have attracted unwanted attention), often failed to bring water and food to the barn. Judging by the entries in the diary, the fear and the hunger went hand in hand with the ever-present boredom of living enclosed in a box, in unending darkness. With time, Melania and Helena's attitude toward their "Uncle" — their only link to the outside world — started to change and to evolve. With the exception of rare (and usually rather unpleasant) visits of "our Lady," "Uncle" was the only human being the girls were to see during their years underground. This simple peasant was, at the same time, the man whose good will (or lack thereof) could suddenly and irreversibly change their fate. "Uncle" became, without any exaggeration, the master of their life and death. Slowly, no doubt under "Uncle's" influence, the language of Melania's diary started to change. With time, the entries include more and more expressions taken from rural dialect, which replaced the literary Polish used by Melania in the ghetto and during the first months of hiding. Despite her very young age, Melania knew full well that her fate hinged on the humour and whims of the "Uncle," who now acquired a new nickname — "Ciuruniu" — that referred to the words "my little daughter" (*córuniu*), which he used when addressing the two girls.

In the fall of 1943, Melania wrote about "Ciuruniu": "… *due…to his own indomitable desire and his willingness to save the poor human souls, this noble soul has overcome countless obstacles at every step and is trying to prolong our miserable life in all possible and impossible ways. Ciuruniu, our life. Be strong, keep true to your decision, which is a most difficult one to fulfill! If at least some of your dreams, so primitive and modest, could come true!*" It was around that time that one of Ciuruniu's "primitive and modest dreams" came true and he started to have sex with Helena. In order to describe the sexual intercourse, Melania invented a new word in her Polish vocabulary (*lutanie*), which henceforth was to appear in the diary with increasing frequency. Their own bodies were the girls' last possession, the last thing they could offer to their saviour. Sex with Helena not only provided Ciuruniu with additional incentive to continue his sacrifice and to shelter the girls, but it also introduced change to the otherwise deadly monotony of life underground. In December 1943, Melania made the following note in her diary: "*I convinced her to provoke Ciuruniu, to let him know that she was also willing, despite the cold. She listened to me and she let him know and it happened. And we have such a pleasant topic for another couple of days.*"

Nevertheless, with time, Melania's and Helena's situation continued to deteriorate. In Dąbrowa Tarnowska and its vicinity, peasants took part in manhunts for hidden Jews. In July 1943, someone informed the Germans about the Jews hidden in Szarwark, a hamlet a few miles away from Wójcik's farm. The German gendarmes, having received precise information about the identity of the alleged rescuers, arrived in the village, murdered the denounced Polish family and set the farm on fire. The local Polish peasants, terrorized and fearing for their own families, began to murder on their own the last surviving Jews. In this "task" they drew upon the assistance of the Polish "Blue" Police. Under these circumstances, sheltering Jews (or even offering them other, short-lived, forms of assistance) carried special risks and was incomparably more dangerous than other signs of defiance against German rule. The continued presence of two Jewish girls became, soon enough, a horrible burden to Ciuruniu and his sister who, time and again, wanted to get rid of the unwanted guests. Throwing the Jews out was, however, a dangerous option, too. In case of capture — and once in the open Jews did not last long — the girls would be forced to talk and would reveal the location of their previous shelter. Such a turn of events was even more frightening for their Polish hosts than the dangers associated with keeping Melania and Helena in the box under the barn.

Sometime near the end of 1943 or in the winter of 1944, Melania also started to have sex with Ciuruniu. The brief entries in the diary in which thirteen-year-old Melania describes sex with her forty-year-old rescuer are something unique in Holocaust literature. It may even be the only description of this kind that has been preserved. The entries, which require empathy and careful reading (often reading between the lines of the diary), with their horrible background and horrifying consequences, extend beyond the normal interpretations of human behaviour. The sometimes playful descriptions of sex cannot hide the realities the two half-starved girls experience — everyday misery, fear and absolute dependence on their host.

Every page of the diary brings further evidence of the cold, hunger and distress that marked every passing day underground. Ciuruniu's mood changes threw both helpless girls to the bottom of despair. From time to time the girls wrote letters to their rescuer (who had acquired a new nickname: The Rascal, or *Huncwot*), in which they tried to seduce him, to make him once again interested in them. Their dramatic fight for survival — for an additional half-rotten apple, for another mouthful of water, for a handful of potato peels — lasted until the final days of the war.

In the summer of 1944, the girls thought that liberty was right around the corner when the Soviet advance pushed the Germans back as far as Radomyśl Wielki, a town about fifteen kilometres away. And there the eastern front stabilized — for the next endless six months. As late as January 1945, barely a few days before the Soviet offensive that was to liberate Dąbrowa Tarnowska, Melania and Helena were convinced that their last moment had come. Melania even thought about blackmailing "The Rascal" with her alleged pregnancy. She did not have to: the next day the Soviet army broke through the German defenses and seized the area. Ciuruniu brought the good news to the hideout but told the girls to stay put and stay in the barn, at least until nightfall. The last thing "The Rascal" wanted was his neighbours learning about the fact that he had sheltered Jews. He also requested that in the future the girls keep this information to themselves.

Ciuruniu was no fool — many Poles who had sheltered Jews during the war were murdered or robbed after liberation. The attackers were, most often, looking for the fabled "Jewish gold" that, it was assumed, the Jews must have left behind as payment for services rendered during the occupation.

After spending a short time in Dąbrowa, Melania returned to Krakow, where she went to a school for Jewish children. In 1946, after the notorious Kielce pogrom in which a mob killed forty-two Jewish survivors of the Holocaust, Melania fled to Germany. In 1948, together with one thousand other Jewish orphans, she immigrated to Canada. Helena (now Helen) eventually found her way to the United States. Today, Molly (in Canada Melania changed her name) lives in Toronto, surrounded by her children, grandchildren and great-grandchildren. Decades after the war, in the late 1990s, Molly described anew her wartime experiences for the benefit of her children and grandchildren, this time in English. Her memoir is reproduced in the present volume, after the diary.

With the passage of time it is natural for us to suppress our most painful memories and instead focus on more positive aspects of the past. It is not surprising, therefore, that during the late 1980s Melania made an appeal to Yad Vashem Institute in Jerusalem to recognize the wartime sacrifice of Ciuruniu and his sister. Her voice was heard and, in 1992, Wiktor Wójcik and Eugenia Kułaga were awarded the medals of Righteous Among the Nations. Naturally, the sanitized version of events submitted to Yad Vashem authorities is markedly different from what can be found in Melania's diary. The evidence collected by the Department of the Righteous of Yad Vashem is not intended to shed light on the past; its goal is to provide evidence that will enable the Institute to award the prestigious medals.

Melania's diary should encourage us to deeply reflect upon the essence of rescue, the limits of sacrifice and the complexity of human motives. It should also be a warning against simplistic interpretations of the stories of the Righteous. Molly (Melania) even today fondly remembers her saviours, Wójcik and Eugenia, and she is still in regular correspondence with their children and grandchildren. Every few weeks she sends them an envelope with a fifty-dollar bill stuffed inside. And she has been doing it for the last fifty years.

Jan Grabowski
University of Ottawa
2017

SOURCES AND SUGGESTIONS FOR FURTHER READING:

Adelson, Alan, ed., and Kamil Turowski, trans. *The Diary of Dawid Sierakowiak: Five Notebooks from the Lodz Ghetto.* New York: Oxford University Press, 1996.

Bowman, Derek, trans. *The Diary of Dawid Rubinowicz.* Edmonds, Wash.: Creative Options Publishing, 1982.

Grabowski, Jan. *Hunt for the Jews.* Bloomington, IN: Indiana University Press, 2013.

Gross, Jan T. *Golden Harvest: Events at the Periphery of the Holocaust.* Oxford and New York: Oxford University Press, 2012.

Gutman, Israel, and Shmuel Krakowski. *Unequal Victims: Poles and Jews during World War Two.* New York: Holocaust Library, 1986.

Holliday, Laurel. *Children in the Holocaust and World War II: Their Secret Diaries.* New York: Pocket Books, 1995.

Ringelblum, Emanuel. *Polish–Jewish Relations during the Second World War.* New York: Fertig, 1976.

Shneiderman, S.L., ed. *The Diary of Mary Berg: Growing Up in the Warsaw Ghetto.* Oxford: Oneworld, 2006.

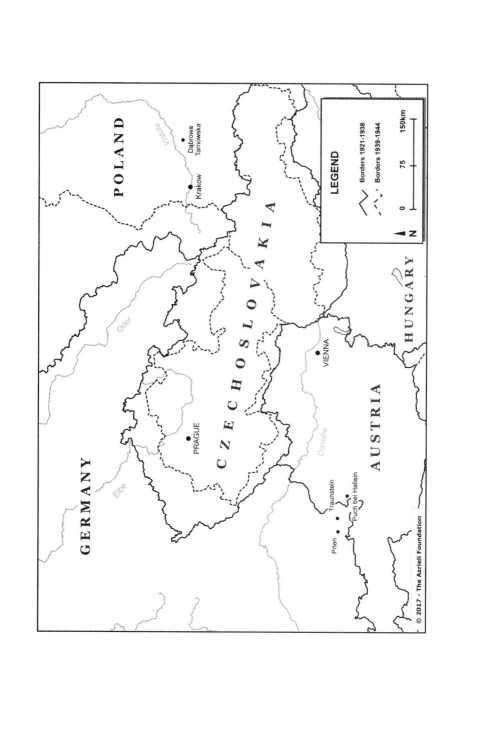

POLAND

Vistula

Dąbrowa Tarnowska

Krakow

GERMANY

Oder

Elbe

C Z E C H O S L O V A K I A

PRAGUE

VIENNA

Danube

AUSTRIA

HUNGARY

Traunstein

Prien

Puch bei Hallein

LEGEND

Borders 1921-1938

Borders 1939-1944

0   75   150km

N

© 2017 – The Azrieli Foundation

Part One: Molly's Diary

w miarę możności dotrzymać słowa. Jeżeli będę tylko miała jakąś tajemnicę, to Ci ją zaraz powierzę, bo wiem, że bez tego nie może istnieć prawdziwa przyjaźń

Lecz to co chowam na dnie mojego jeszcze bardzo dziecinnego serduszka, muszę nawet i przed Tobą mój pamiętniczku niestety zataić. „To" jest tak wielkie i razem tak głupie, że boję się je nawet Tobie pamiętniczku powierzyć. Bo a nuż ktoś niezaproszony trafi do Ciebie i przeczyta zawarte w Tobie słowa, a już jestem zdradzona. „Tego" nie powierzyłam jeszcze nikomu i zdaje się, że nikomu nigdy nie powiem. Zresztą „to" są przecież tylko moje myśli i przypuszczenia.

Dn. 1/III 1942

Naprawdę, nie wiedziałam, że pisanie pamiętnika jest tak wielką przyjemnością.

The first page of Molly's diary. March 1, 1942.

1942

... I will try to be true to my word[1]... If I have any secret at all I shall confide it in you immediately, because I know that there can be no true friendship without that. But the "thing" I'm hiding at the bottom of my still very childish heart, unfortunately, must be concealed even from you, my diary. This "thing" is so great and at the same time so silly that I'm afraid to confide even in you, my diary. This is because if someone finds you and reads the words written in you, then I shall immediately be exposed. I have not confided this "thing" to anybody and it seems that I never will...

Sunday, March 1
I really had no idea that writing a diary is such a great pleasure, and it does not seem too late now at all. I look at each written page with respect. Why, these are the pages of my existence, my life. I would like to write a couple of words every day, but I doubt it shall be possible. The time alone is to blame. I am busy doing nothing all day long and in the evening I cannot [write], because of the dark and cold. The obstacles keep mounting. But I am not to blame. Now, as I am writing by a kerosene lamp, my eyes are heavy with sleep.

Oh, it is already so late...

---

1 The first pages of the diary were lost.

Tuesday, March 10

What a pity that I was born in the century assigned for fighting great battles! Why did it happen to me? When I was little I dreamt that my life would turn out happy and carefree. How stupid it seems to me now... and how unreachable it is. When I looked at the world with the eyes of a child it appeared so rose-coloured... and now? I am happy when I survive another day, and I await the next in fear. When is it going to end? Are we even going to live until the end? It is very, very doubtful. Sometimes when I wake at night and reflect upon it I see what this war has already done. What a toll it has taken and how much blood and how many tears have been shed. And what is still to come? This question is the worst. I cannot write about it anymore. Even though one would not know by looking at me, I am very worried. Perhaps a brighter day will come tomorrow (for today was awful) and I will write more.

Tuesday, March 17

Oh God, I nurse such a grievance against You.... Why do You let such terrible atrocities occur? Instead of complaining or moaning I have been thankful for everything. Yes, for everything. Even for things nobody else would think of. But now, Oh God! I am forced to beg you, even though I know that my request will not reach Your divine ears, for immediately above the ground it will intersect with a completely opposite request and after a short struggle they will both fall to the ground. And from thence there is no return.

But I will try anyway. For everybody who sends a request knows that it will not reach the Almighty. But they send it anyway. Why? Because they hope. Why, I live hoping, too, so today I send my pleas away into the vast distance. And I shall wait for benevolent God to hear me. My request is passionate and as dear as life is dear to every man. I ask of You, God, do not let us die; liberate us from the hands of our tormentors. God, let us live peacefully until the end of our existence. Forgive us our sins, which are as great as Your punishment is severe. Unite everybody whom You have separated and make them happy until the end of their lives!

Saturday, March 21

Mela, Melusia,[2] spring is coming. Yes, it must be her. Believe it or not, I hear the rustle of her transparent wings and I see her golden dress woven from rays of sunshine. And what is that on her head? Oh, it is a crown of primroses — her first harbingers. She is coming, walking slowly like a turtle for one, or silently like a butterfly for another, or running nimbly like a small deer for yet another.

She is already here. She came to me when she crossed the threshold of our tiny room. No, not the threshold, but the windowsill, for she came in through the window with a gust of wind. She looks into every corner, every nook and cranny and every hole; simply, everywhere. And she is so innocent and her soul so pure, that wherever she looks it becomes cheerful and pleasant there. And the sadness goes away.

Spring, sweet spring! Do not forget, remember and look everywhere. It becomes bright wherever you look and the sadness disappears.

You have already gone... you went to other homes, to other people. And you failed to look everywhere. For you forgot to look into our dark, miserable, unhappy Jewish souls.

Monday, March 30

So what? So what that spring is already here, that the snow is melting, that the sun is shining warmer, that animals are waking from hibernation and the birds will soon return from southern climates; so what that our holidays finally start the day after tomorrow?

So what? Marie Vetsera and her beloved Rudolf cannot see that.[3] Just yesterday I obtained a book with the title Mayerling[4] and I find it fascinating, to the extent that I dreamt about them last night. Even

---

2 Mela and Melusia are nicknames for Melania, the author's birth name.

3 A reference to Crown Prince Rudolf of Austria and his mistress, Baroness Maria Vetsera. In 1889, the lovers were found dead in an apparent murder-suicide at the Prince's hunting lodge, Mayerling.

4 *Mayerling* was written by Claude Anet (a pseudonym of Jean Schopfer) in 1930.

though it is a popular story, I had never heard about the two of them. I pity them so much. Why did they do that? I think that they should not have done it. The beautiful, petite Marie would be seventy today and Rudolf would be an eighty-five-year-old man. Even though they would have been married throughout those years, I think that they wouldn't have been happy. So maybe it is better that they left this world with a feeling of happiness?

Monday, April 13
If only you knew, Bineczka,[5] how much I love you... Oh, if only you knew. But you do not and you shall never know. Because you will not believe that such a love can exist. It is called lesbian love; that is, of a woman for another woman. I love you with all my naive, still entirely pure, tiny heart. And I am suffering. And you are my first love. What a pity that I cannot give you telling proofs of my love! Consequently, the ones I can give must suffice. If only I could do something for you...

But you do not ask anything of me, because you do not think me capable of anything.

But do know this, my beloved Bineńka, my love for you can accomplish much. Remember that you can always count on me, no matter what.

Monday, April 20
Even though just a couple of days ago I wrote about spring, I feel an urge to write something about it again, for we are alive in the most beautiful season...

Spring! This one tiny word: spring! Such charm it holds! Spring, sweet spring! How beautiful, divine and charming you are! We liken

---

5   Molly refers to Sabina Goldman, the object of her affection, using a number of terms of endearment, such as Bineczka, Binusia, Binka, which have been retained in the translation.

everything that is good and beautiful to you. Happiness — this is spring, love — this is spring, youth — this is spring.

Happy are those who breathe in your fragrance, those whom you delight with the beauty of your visage. Happy? Yes, happy. But [only] those for whom no cloud obscures their view, who can take delight in your beauty. Yet for us? Your radiant sun does not shine for us, nor does the grass turn green for us, nor do the blue skies smile on us. A black, impenetrable cloud is hanging over our heads. Is it always going to be thus? Are there no winds that would disperse it? Or perhaps you, bright, innocent spring, are able to penetrate these thick, dark clouds? And maybe then the sun would finally shine for us?

Wednesday, April 29

How naive were my thoughts! I can see this only now. I had thought until this last awful moment, that there is — I mean that here, in this case, there would be — a place between the mouth and the edge of the chalice.[6]... But I can see that there is not. And I can also see something else, there, in the distance, through a tiny crack, where hardly anybody comes and where surely nobody looks but me, I saw..., that there is nobody there, high above, over our heads, and higher still, above the clouds. There, in heaven. Neither an angel, nor even a[n angel's] wing. Nothing. My faith in the Almighty, who purportedly sits there, has long been weak. And today it shattered. It is possible that at the moment when I was looking my eyes deceived me so I will not say the final word until I am absolutely sure.

Sunday, June 21

My sweet Aleczka!

---

6 *Between the Mouth and the Edge of the Chalice* is the title of a well-known Polish novel by Maria Rodziewiczówna. Originally published in 1889, the book, a classic love story, was very popular reading in the 1920s and 1930s.

Even though I do not know what awaits me tomorrow I pity you so much... I do not know. I have no idea how my later life without you shall be. Sweet Fredzio! Dearest Aleczka![7] And the rest of you! Where are you? Are you alive? Oh, there is no higher being either on the globe or above it than man! There is not! How horrible this is! Nobody can comprehend it unless they experience it themselves. That is how it is.

Saturday, July 25
Last night I slept with Bineczka in the attic. A couple more nights like that and we will be in the cemetery.[8]

Friday, August 7
It was Bineczka's birthday yesterday. I presented her with a bouquet of flowers and I wrote her a letter. She threw a party at her girlfriend's and invited all her girl and boy friends plus her acquaintances. She excluded me, of course. She received a couple of attractive presents and was offered many good wishes, but surely none were as true and sincere as mine.

Sunday, August 9
I was at Binka's this morning and I immediately noticed that something was troubling her, even though she was seemingly smiling and even cheerful. So I began asking her questions and insisted that she reveal

---

7   Aleczka (Aleksandra) and Fredzio (Alfred) are Molly's cousins.
8   During the liquidation actions Melania went into hiding in the attic of her house. In June, the Germans imposed a levy on Jewish inhabitants of Dąbrowa Tarnowska, allegedly to shield them against deportation. Despite the payment of the levy, the first liquidation action took place at the end of June and several hundred Jews were taken from the ghetto and later sent to Bełżec. On July 17, another action took place: this time more than 1,000 Jews were taken to the Bełżec death camp. Expecting more deportations, people started to build ingenious hideouts in their houses in the ghetto, in order to weather the storm.

the reason for her sadness. In the end she told me that on the day of her birthday one of the girls she knew, an Ania W., looked at her palm and then refused to say a word. Since that girl is apparently a competent palmist, now Binka thinks that she saw an ill omen — purportedly her lifeline will soon break. That was the reason [for her mood]. *Binka plans to go to that girl tomorrow and insist that she tell her the truth. Oh, how I worry about her life!*

Monday, August 10
Today I was waiting impatiently for the moment when I could ask my beloved Binka what that Ania W. had told her. But because she was in a much better mood than yesterday I suspected that the girl must have made a mistake. Then Binusia told me that Ania gave her hope that she would survive the war, and that she cared about nothing else because she only wanted to see the end of the war, so she was happy again.
All this seems very unclear. I am very frightened.

Sunday, August 16
I have a bad premonition. An enormous, black cloud is hanging over us and it surely shall descend on us. Why would you try to convince yourself that it shall not do so, that enough has already happened and that nothing else will? Why, Dąbrowa is no different, no better town than any other! The people who live here are as diverse as anywhere else. There are the good and the bad, the jealous and the merciful, the poor and the better-off, the happy and the unhappy. So why would you try to convince yourself that a miracle is going to happen before they [the Germans] *manage to do something bad? If there were miracles, then we would have already seen something. There has been so much evil! And if there were miracles and they could do something good then they would surely not tolerate human suffering, which is indeed boundless, with indifference! And soon there shall not be anybody left to suffer!*

Friday, September 4

It has already been a week since I last saw Bineńka. Today I could not stand it any longer and I walked to her house because I knew that she had returned from the Gemeinschaft, the municipality office where she works as a secretary.[9] But it seems that she was not pleased with my visit and that she had not missed me at all, as I had missed her. I did not wish to bore her too long and so I went home, even though I would have been very happy to look at her for a little longer because I have a feeling that the good shall not last long now. I hope my intuition is wrong.

Wednesday, September 9

What I had dreaded the most has finally happened. I must part from my dearest Bineńka. Oh, how horrible this is! I shall never, ever see her again! What shall I do without her? Who am I going to turn to in times of doubt or grievance against the entire world? It is a most severe blow for me... There are only a couple more hours left! So I will write her a farewell letter because I cannot say what I feel toward her and what I wish for her future, which I hope she will live to have! It is the end. It is over. The soap bubble has burst. I did not expect that we would part in such conditions. Bineńka was weeping with sorrow while reading my letter and she held my head in her hands for so long, looking into my eyes. I demanded a blessing from her and she did bless me. I am leaving town, never to return again. Nothing good has ever happened to me here. I lost all my family members whom I loved and finally today I must leave Bineńka, the creature I love the most in the world. I shall spend the first days waiting for what may be the last letter from her, but I do not know what I shall do even then.

---

9 Sabina worked in the office of Jewish Social Self-Help (Żydowska Samopomoc Społeczna).

Thursday, September 10

I am living at a certain peasant woman's, where I hide with my family from the storm, which has to pass over the town.[10] Oh, how I worry about my love, who stayed in that awful town! I have whole days to myself so I cannot help thinking a lot. I shudder to think that Bineczka might not leave the town in time!

Saturday, September 12

Today I received a letter from my beloved Bineńka, on which I shed bitter [tears].[11] For how can one accept the thought that it is already our end, that we are seventy years old, despite being in our prime, despite being only twenty years old! If only we might see each other again!

Thursday, September 17

Father came to us today, as the situation in town has become horrible. It was with such a heavy heart that I accepted the news that my dear Binka was sitting in some dungeon, awaiting the worst. How she must be suffering there, the poor thing! Why, Bineczka, you said that you would not go anywhere, that you would not part from your parents! You must count on your lucky star and on me. I might be able to do something anyway, because I will try to help you with all my strength. If only I were in town I would surely succeed!

---

10 Anticipating the next liquidation action, Melania's mother arranged for her daughter to leave the ghetto and move to the barn on the farm of Wiktor (Victor) Wójcik and his sister, Eugenia (Emilia) Kułaga.

11 Melania preserved Sabina's letter throughout the war. An image of the letter is reproduced in the photo section, which begins on page 127; the letter's translation appears in the second part of this volume.

Friday, September 18
It has been such a horrible day in town today![12] *Not even one Jew left. All of them have been deported to die! What is my Bineńka doing? What would I not do to be able to have her beside me? Why, she must be still alive! There has been nothing to suggest otherwise.*

Saturday, September 19
Today in the afternoon, while I was sitting in the barn as usual, I heard a crow cawing. It perched over my head for a long time, its cawing so menacing, that I had the impression that something evil would befall me at that very moment. And it seemed strange to me, that none but I heard that cawing. What could it mean?

Sunday, September 20
I had a disturbing dream last night. No, not disturbing, but I am almost sure that, oh, something bad has happened to my sweet, dearest Bineczka. I dreamt that her mother was sitting in the kitchen and ordered her to fry a little chicken for her. So Binka caught it and put a knife to its throat. Standing right by her, I watched what she was doing. When I saw her walking up to that little chicken to kill it I quickly turned away because I could not bear the sight. After a while I turned around and saw the chicken, already dead, standing calmly with its throat cut, as if nothing had happened. There was no trace of blood. I even tried to chase the chicken, but it only moved a little from where it was standing, its eyelid strangely covering its eyeball. And that was what I dreamt.

Oh, how dreadfully miserable I am!

---

12 The final, brutal, liquidation of the Dąbrowa ghetto took place on September 18, 1942. The German "liquidation commando" and the Polish "Blue" Police both took part in the action. More than one thousand Jews were taken to the Bełżec death camp and hundreds of others were killed in the streets of Dąbrowa Tarnowska and in the local Jewish cemetery.

Tuesday, September 22

Father is supposed to return to town tonight, for we have had no news. Why, we had nobody to obtain information from. Even though I fear that something bad might happen to him, I hope that all shall be well, because he is truly fortune's favourite. Oh, how I wish that he had already sent a note or come in person, so that I might finally learn what ails my dearest Bineczka, whom I love the most in the world.

Oh, I'm already going crazy...

Wednesday, September 23

Yes. The thing I so dreaded must have already happened. It is already a fact. For I knew, I was simply sure, that my great love would give me a sign if anything bad happened.

If someone were to read these words, he would think that the writer was deranged and that in her madness she had recalled a fairy tale about a brother who had set out on a journey, having left his sister a necklace of coral pieces, which would ooze blood, or something similar, in the case of his death. And I have just lost the main gem in the ring I received a year ago from Bineczka, which has been my talisman. That glass gem was like Binka's heart. And so her little heart has been torn out!!!

Monday, September 28

Sadly all my premonitions have proved to be true! If only that dreadful day when I learned from Father's letter that my dearest, most beloved creature in the world had been deported to certain death had never come.[13] Then, having electrocuted her, they will suck out the fat for soap! Oh, it is horrid beyond imagination! To cut the stems of such young,

---

13 Sabina Goldman had tried to flee from the Dąbrowa train station and had been caught by the Polish "Blue" Police. The "Blues" transferred Sabina to the Germans, who added her to the death transport leaving for Bełżec.

beautiful flowers! If I live to avenge it, how terrible and cruel my vengeance will be! It is for that vengeance that I suffer and live the life of a true martyr. That is all that keeps me alive. When will that reckoning come?

Sunday, October 11

Oh, how heavy are the hearts of those who do not believe in the Almighty! I would have never said that had I not experienced it myself... And now, in the face of certain death, I have nobody to turn to in my final hours, nobody to ask for mercy, nor even for consolation. If my love were alive, which I very, very much doubt, I would go to her and after her words my fear of death would surely no longer be so terrible. How I regret now that I am parted from her! Why, death at her side would be sweet and easy! What good has it done me that I did not go with her? Perhaps only that I have one more month to worry about this awful thing they call life. And it seems that the only benefit was that I was able to mourn her, without even knowing what death she died and what happened to her most precious remains! But there shall be nobody to mourn me... Bineczka! You were the only one I believed in and you were my Goddess! So if there is an afterlife and if your soul has soared somewhere into the air and if your soul is capable, I am begging you: make it so that I may stay alive for a while longer. I wish to continue to live for some time to be able to avenge your death. Then I will leave this world with the feeling that I have done everything that I should. And then? Oh, then we will unite forever, for eternal life and I will be with my Bineńka forever!

Wednesday, October 14

My heart is made of stone or steel. And if there is a material that is harder still, then it is precisely what my heart is made of. Because otherwise I could not bear the thought that I shall never ever see my father or brother again. For when one falls into the clutches, it is impossible to get out. Am I [really] bearing it too? How strange it is that one can bear so much... This must be something superhuman. Oh, I cannot write any more!

Friday, October 16
Dearest Binuś! I am writing to you, while relieving my pain with my other hand.

Death has taken you from me — I am alone now. Dearest Binuś, I am writing to you...

Wednesday, October 21
What a happy day Mother had yesterday! And obviously I did, too, even though few things affect me, either the bad or the good. For I take everything with an indifferent and slightly ironic expression on my face. When Father and Zyga[14] were deported to Tarnów on Wednesday I did not expect to ever hear from them at all. But to our surprise, we received a letter from them yesterday. It is neither bad nor good, but they are alive and that is what counts. Everything else is secondary. But will 'the good' last?

...I have been feeling a strange urge today to examine my treasure. And now I must take a look at it. I will also write down and conceal in it what I fear to confide even in you, my dearest diary. [?]

[...] It will be difficult for the Jews to stay alive until New Year. For a present, I was given a wheat pancake, a potato pancake, a couple of baked potatoes and pickled tomatoes. And Mother and Helcia[15] gave me their best wishes. If only they could give me their best wishes again! If I survive until the New Year, my faith in God will begin to return.

Bineczka, watch over me!

---

14 Melania's younger brother.
15 Helcia is a nickname for Helen, Melania's cousin.

Friday, October 27
*Zyga returned from Tarnów today! He escaped from a transport he was
in with our papa, and after several adventures came to our barn by
train. I do not feel like reporting his adventures, because my diary is
already rather frightening.*

Tuesday, December 8
*Cold and grim wind is blowing, it snows sharply on my eyes, the black
heavens obscured by clouds, my soul is quiet and dark. I'm terrified,
terrified... I only hear my trembling and my pained sobs and weeps.
I want to [see] you Binka, you... My beloved Binka is gone, the Binka
I loved so much, the only [comfort] is that I, ah, said goodbye to her.
Goodbye, goodbye...*

*My Binka, Binka, have you gone somewhere far, far away, or have
you left me forever. Tell me, do tell me, my heart is crying, because I'll
never see my little Binka again. Never, never again...*

Sunday, December 20
*This was the worst, the most horrible night in my entire life so far. I
would not wish such a torment even on my enemy. The separation from
Mummy and Zyga was unbelievably painful and horrible.*[16]

Tuesday, December 22
The policemen are finished.[17]

---

16 The Polish farmers who were hiding Melania and her family, afraid of the risks
   associated with sheltering them, refused to keep her brother any longer. After
   the war, Melania was able to find out only that her mother had been killed in the
   Tarnów ghetto. Nothing is known about the fate of her brother and her stepfather.
17 The last Jews still living in what was, until September 1942, the Dąbrowa Tarnowska ghetto (some thirty Jewish policemen and their families) remained
   locked up in one of the ghetto houses. On December 20, 1942, they were shot
   in the Jewish cemetery by the local gendarmes under the command of Rudolf

Tuesday, December 29
When bitter winter roams the world
And chilly wind blows in the hideout
No one can stop this cold
Because all evil is hell bent.

My dream is a quilt
To cover myself from head to toe.
A girl has different dreams
When warmth helps her fall asleep.

Grim days and freezing nights;
This is, after all, humanity's foe.
When all the body shivers and trembles
One cannot heat up the cold legs.

And though the holes are covered
To heat the night at least a little,
And though our stomachs are full,
Strength's no good for a quilt.

Useless [are] *coats and furs*
If there were a hundred of them.
Nothing's better than a quilt's down
Because it relieves the evil cold.

Landgraf. Even Kalman Fenichel, the much-hated chief of the Jewish police, was unable to save his own life and was executed along with his ten-year-old son and the rest of his subordinates. Stanisław Dorosz from Dąbrowa — possibly the only witness to this execution — watched the shooting hidden in a shed, some forty metres away from the place of the killings: "They [the gendarmes] marched them out of the house four by four and led them to the Jewish cemetery. There, they told them to strip and to jump into the pits, which had been dug earlier. A Gestapo agent from Tarnów did the shooting. He shot all the Jews the same way."

All speculation useless
To heat oneself, useless toil.
All imitation useless
Even if there were plenty.

Useless straw, useless hay
It seems only a nobleman
Can get warm.
But that's not enough in Poland.

O my nice quilt
Everyone does know about it.
That when your down is there,
I'll heat up through and through.

1943

Thursday, January 7
I do not write, because my hands are cold.

Monday, January 25
A major change in my life! We changed our 'accommodation' today. We moved from the hideout in the barn to a box buried in the ground. It has a hole for light and air to come in, but we cannot sit in it. Lying idly for a whole day is horrible, for it is only at night when we can go out, stretch out in the stinking cold dark stable and shudder whenever we hear a dog bark. But it feels delightful, for our bones ache after an entire day spent lying. But how long can we stand in that darkness, cold and stench? Chilled to the bone and dead tired, after two hours we crawl back into our den, where we have our eiderdown and pillow. At six o'clock in the morning we crawl back out to wash ourselves a bit and relieve ourselves. After we go back in we lie there until night. In the evening we crawl back out and so on. My Kitten[18] is the sweetest in the entire world. Is she not? [illegible crossed-out word] *All this intermingles with fear and less pleasant announcements made by 'uncle'* [Victor],

---

18 "Kitten" is a translation of the Polish diminutive *Kotuśka*. This is how Melania refers to her cousin Helena (Helen).

such as that they [the Nazis] *found a Jewish family somewhere and executed them! This is what they call luck, a stroke of luck indeed. And we should thank God a hundred times a day that it is as it is and no different. And we keep praying for the health of our beloved, kind landlords — our 'uncle' and our lady — so that they can successfully adhere to their noble intention. If only God would give them strength to be steadfast with us! Because these people with hearts of gold are doing everything they can and are capable of for us. I still admire their perseverance, because this is no mean feat and after all they have no obligations toward us, because before we came to them they did not even know us that well! I feel that they often dislike us, for we are the reason for their fear and the anxiety they have been living in since we came to them. But their exemplary character prevents them from sending us to certain death and their deep faith in God helps them overcome the panicky fear, which unfortunately, often takes place. Dear, beloved 'uncle' with a heart of gold and you, our sweet lady! How boundlessly grateful I am that you are helping us push this awfully heavy wheelbarrow of life, on which bad people have put such a heavy burden that I surely would not be able to push it without you, no matter how much I would try!*

Thursday, February 18
It's the 18th again! I cannot stand this date; I hate it.[19] *Everything bad has something to do with the number 18. But to be honest, for us every day is as horrible and awful as any other. But this 18th inspires a particular fear in me. It has already been five months since I last was on the surface of the earth. These months have caused me so much pain, oh, so much! If only the coming months would bring me something better! For spring is coming... Oh, spring...*

*   While you, a decent person, have to rot* [here] *despite being still 'alive.'*

---

19 The ghetto in Dąbrowa Tarnowska was liquidated on September 18, 1942.

Monday, February 22

My dear diary! I need to confess that for a while I have not been as honest with you as I should have. But you will forgive me because you know why that was. You know that instead of laying my thoughts on your pages I was writing letters to Bineczka. But unfortunately, I cannot do that anymore, because you know that she has already gone. If you, my diary, were a young girl, I would tell you something in secret, but as you are not, I will write down what I would otherwise whisper to you.

With her thirteen virtues, Helcia is beginning to keep secrets from me. Pish, I dislike that, though she may well be right. I am still foolish and I do not know anything. This is precisely why she should show me these pieces of paper. Why, I need to find out eventually. But I will not insist if she does not want to. Who knows? It might be better for me this way. My diary, answer me...

Sunday, March 14

I have opened my notebook again after a rather long break. And it is because today we are standing for the whole day in the stable to stretch ourselves out a little. And because it is very uncomfortable for me to write lying down, I brought the notebook upstairs. But the conditions are not favourable here either, because I am chilled to the bone even though it is mid-March and the weather is beautiful, the sun is shining brightly and the earth is fragrant. If only I could walk out of the stable door and sit on the threshold... It is so distant and simply unattainable, that, unfortunately, I should not even whet my appetite and dream about it. I already cannot imagine a life different from the one I am living. Shall it always be like this? Is the evil ever going to end?

Wednesday, April 7

The world is so large, so extremely enormous, that you cannot go around it fast or comprehend its vastness, not even with your mind. Almost the entire globe is inhabited by people. Apparently people live even on the other side of the moon and on Mars, too. There is a place on the surface of the earth for all living creatures. Sadly, there is no place on the surface of the earth only for two miserable, abandoned living creatures. So these two poor, miserable human beings are forced to live under the surface, squeezed in a small box, where you can merely lie down and still feel cramped. And you can only dream about sitting. And these creatures lie in this box for months on end and they emerge into the stable for only three hours a day. Confinement — dirt, bugs, darkness and stuffiness — as in a grave. But these creatures are so happy that it is as it is and not worse and they are thankful for this 'grave' in their daily prayers. And they say nothing, they do not even complain anymore because they know that there is no place for them on the surface of the earth. Are we destined to ever emerge onto the surface?

Friday, April 16
My eye is hurting... And I have nobody to lick it clean. Helcia doesn't want to because she is scared that she shall become infected. Don't worry, Helcia. If you do and your eye is festering as mine is today, I will lick it clean for you. But on the condition it is as feline as mine. And I will lick away your holy tears, too. I wish that your eye would start hurting already.

Friday, April 23
Oh, you silly, you fool... How do you imagine it? Do you think that I'm serious when I say that I will not give you any? How can you think so? Why, if I were to eat something better than you, it would stick in my throat. Do you believe also that I would not give you exactly half of the hemp seeds? When you made that promise back then, I immediately had no intention to [ever] hold you to it. I just wish to test you, like Griselda from the fairy tale.

Thursday, May 20
I am terribly bored. Helcia and I no longer have anything to talk about because we ran out of topics a long time ago. For we have been inseparable for a month and devoid of new sensations. Oh, I am so terribly

bored... I would write on your pages, my diary, but as I have only sad thoughts circling in my head I do not wish to write them down in a diary. I have nothing to do at all. Oh, if only I could go out onto the surface...

Oh, vain hopes, unattainable, elusive...

Tuesday, September 21
This moron does not let me write, even though I often wish to. But when she shall not see, I'll fill all until the last page. All right? My dearest kitten, good night.

Sunday, October 10
Sex.

Wednesday, October 27
If somebody had told me exactly a year ago that I would live to see another year I should have never believed him, even if he were considered and regarded as most sensible. It has been no mean feat and an achievement of our 'Cyril Falls.'[20] I believe that due not so much to his noble deeds as to his own indomitable desire and his willingness to save the poor human souls, this noble soul has overcome countless obstacles at every step and is trying to prolong our miserable life in all possible and impossible ways. Ciuruniu, our life.[21] Be strong to adhere to your intention, which is a most difficult one to fulfill! If at least some of your dreams, so primitive and modest, could come true!

On each birthday, that is, for about ten years, I like to sum up the past year. Actually, the last year passes before my eyes of its own volition, from the beginning to the end, like a colour film, its frames diverse and changing like in a kaleidoscope.

---

20 Cyril Falls (1888–1971) was a well-known British military historian and writer.

21 "Ciuruniu" (from *córuniu* — my little daughter) is the new nickname Melania has given to her rescuer.

Oh, how much the last year of my life differs from a colour film and the colourful pieces of glass in a kaleidoscope. If one insisted on looking at the past year of my life through a kaleidoscope I would have to put in it exclusively black pieces of glass, bristling with sharp points, making unpleasant, interrupted sounds when they hit one another. Whoever regards himself as being a very bad past ... I will leave it unfinished...

November
On the first day, terrible fear. Fortunately, nothing happened in the end. Sadly, Ciuruniu has not come over even once for a whole month. Kitten had her birthday and I gave her a small bar of soap. But she washed herself with it only once and she has already hidden it away. Anyway, the most bearable time of day are the evenings, when we lie under the warm eiderdown and Kitten tells me various stories, which often make me burst out laughing. When we are upstairs I have something to do again: Pontuś. I feed him all the time and put tidbits away for him. What a pretty rooster!

December
I still find Kitten's evening stories the most bearable. I spend entire days, so unpleasant and filled with torment, looking forward to the moment when we go back in the box and I can listen to those stories. We talk a lot about having sex and Kitten shows me exactly how it is done. I convinced her to provoke Ciuruniu to let him know that she was also willing, despite the cold. She listened to me and she approached him and it happened. And we have such a pleasant topic for another couple of days. On the whole, every evening throughout December, I have been impressed with a beautiful story that Kitten made up about a girl named Amina.

Sunday, December 26
Sex again.

1944-1945

January

On January 12, Kitten wrote the following letter to Ciuruniu: ["]*I am embarrassed to write to you again, fearing that you might think ill of me, but the last time left me with such a terrible yearning. I bet that you think that I had enough? It only provoked my desire. Afterward I relive it all night long, every nerve trembling in me at the very memory. I felt a particularly overwhelming need after the last time because I had not played enough and I wanted to some more... Honey, my dearest, your every touch feels like an electric current, everything vibrates in me and begs for more... Honey, come caress me a little but this time you need to lay me down, because I must feel all of you on me and pressing down against me. Honey, on the tip and with your finger. And that* [sweet?] *hole with an edge. My baby, hold me and quench my thirst, because I want to faint in your strong, virile arms...* ["]

He came over on the 26th, but Kitten had her period, so he came back again on February 3.

February

We are freezing. There has been heavy frost and we have nothing warm to wear but we do not wish to say a word. Furthermore, we have no food and everything is marked by winter. On the 26th Ciuruniu cut off my Pontus' head. And it is entirely her [Helen's] *fault, because she could*

have easily prevented that. But it seemed too trivial to her. Making matters worse, I became superstitious and came to believe that Pontuś needed to live in order to prevent our situation from deteriorating. That was why I gave her [Helen] so much proof of how much I wanted her to plead for him. But she refused and it is too late now. And as if to punish her for that her heart began bothering her on the very same day. She immediately imagined that she was suffering from all kinds of ailments, both the likely and the unlikely. Her suffering was to a greater extent mental than physical, like a punishment for her failure to act on my request, which was so easy to satisfy. I was not afraid of the consequences at all, because sometimes an inner voice tells me something, and when I repeat it, then even though it lacks substantiation, I can still give it credence. And something was indeed whispering to me that it was nothing, that it would pass on its own, because it was a punishment for Pontuś. Because that psychological pain was meant exclusively for her, so I was not worried at all. Besides, everything only half affects us.
My Kitten had fun.

March
Our cup of bitterness became full when thaw water began creeping up into our hideout, even though there was still heavy frost, and our legs are terribly swollen and frostbitten. Fear since March 15 and Ciuruniu is very worried and sad.[22]

April
On April 5 we slept in the stable because we were afraid that the water would have a detrimental effect on our health, but we became so fright-

---

22 In March 1944, several Jews hidden in the vicinity of Dąbrowa were found and executed. In nearby Wóla Mędrzechowska, two women and their children were killed; two other families were discovered in the village of Tonia; and another group of Jews was killed in Bolesław, a few kilometres north of Melania and Helena's hiding place.

ened that we walked back into the water in the middle of the night. Two days later a pitcher of water spilled over us while it was being hand-ed over. After the holidays we changed the straw and instead of lying in water we are lying in mud. We sewed a dress for Bacha [Barbara, Emilia's daughter], *four panties, a blouse, an apron and socks. It is a pleasure for me. My finger was peeling and hurting. And on April 20 Kitten was suffering from weakness of the heart, so I convinced her to invite Ciuruniu over to strengthen it. And she wrote the following note: "If you want to, come over for a while in the evening, because I am lonely and sad." And he did. And there was some* [sex]. *And her heart became stronger right away because she needed it as medicine.*

May
Sex on May 16, but out of resignation.

At the beginning of May we were sewing two dresses for Madam and a shirt for [the] *boy. We have only now stopped suffering from the cold. Finally the breakthrough day of May 17 came. Ciuruniu came over at midday and said that* [a neighbour] *had said that he was keeping Jews in the stable. Consequently, he could no longer take the risk and he told us to do whatever we wanted. He told us to go into the fields even though he was perfectly aware that living in a field is impossible. We went through a couple of horrible hours as we waited for our departure into the field under cover of night, but then a miracle happened and Ciuruniu said that he would take the risk and he ordered us to go into the hole in the barn. We sat there during the day, but in the evening he ordered us to go back because he was even more anxious with us stay-ing there. So we returned to the old place, but that time to bare, damp straw, without a blanket or simply anything. But we still bear in mind that in a field we would have none of that either. Now we have to lie in the box all day long and he lets us out for the night, so we have to stay up all night to take at least a short nap during the day, but during the day one cannot compensate for the hours one did not sleep at night. A person living normally would not even be able to comprehend what it means to make day out of night and vice versa. We are suffering a lot physically and psychologically, because our sole giver of life and practically everything in the world has undergone a major change. Even though he has sufficient reasons, because the risk is much greater and there is also the hopelessness, but what can we, in misery, do? It is all the worse when both parties are in the right. Our situation has become far worse, even though we have had our fair share of suffering.*

On May 24 I wrote a letter to Ciuruniu.
"I would like to ask you to read these few words, which I write here in silent despair, clutching this piece of paper like a straw. I will neither praise nor flatter you here because I know that you dislike that, but you are our saint and what you have been doing for us is a superhuman feat. I would not like to fall foul of you, because you are doing too much already, but I am forced by an extreme need. A week ago I did not expect that we would still be alive today, because if you say one word, our lives will be over. God has taken pity on us again and He lets us breathe. I would like so much to survive but in the current situation it is highly unlikely. Just the last couple of days have exhausted us because whole days spent lying in stuffiness make us weaker and weaker with every passing hour. These could be the final weeks before a change, because even the recent newspapers suggest that these are the decisive moments. So it would be a pity if finally we were to die a tragic death. Hence, I appeal to your noble heart for you to be as kind as to make one more effort for us. We can somehow endure until late afternoon but by 5:00 p.m. we are already so awfully tired. Would it be possible for us to go into the barn and sit there quietly and if it becomes necessary could we get into that barrel or into some other hideout in the barn? It would be in the evening, when the risk is much less. We could hack out a piece of plank in the corner above the trough in the ceiling, because a hole near the window would be visible. In the stable we would cover [the box?] with harrows on our own and in the evening we would walk back into

the stable. The stable door could remain open for a whole day, except for that moment when we would walk into the barn. On colder days we could somehow endure until evening. Why, people are not so extremely mean as to bring misfortune on others and after a while, when they do not notice any movements, the suspicion will pass. You are risking so much, that in my opinion, it would not constitute a greater risk, while for us it would simply be a salvation. I do not seek any comforts; besides, we are resilient to various tests. But this is unbearable. I would never demand this of you because I have no demands but I am forced to by extreme need. I know that I am making a demand that is beyond your power but I am begging you and appealing to your noble heart. Please, think it over carefully and do not turn down my request. In the name of your kindness and selflessness, it is God who must save us. Fate has tied us in such a strange way and even though we all have such a clean conscience and such sinless intentions we are all suffering so terribly that perhaps we will never go through hell. If it is really impossible for you, then let it be as it is now, and we will offer ourselves up to God. Let it be as He wishes, because we prefer to die here than go seeking death. We will not bear a grievance against you and we will continue to bless you."

Oh, God, inspire this ideal man with some joyful thought!

In reply, Ciuruniu told us to stop bothering ourselves with it and endure the situation as it is and that if there were some new developments in the world, the people would focus on them, and then we would again be able to stay on the surface all day. Okay, but how can one endure that?

June
Sex in broad daylight, behind the door on June 1. Also, on the next day. But it was no fun because it was only that. On June 6 we learned about a very important military event. The long-awaited invasion of France has begun. On account of the invasion, this Rascal lets us out at midday. A week after the start of the invasion he underwent a major change

because he thought that would be the solution. But when he sees that it is still nothing, he becomes very discouraged and his attitude toward us has changed for the worse. He no longer makes sure that we have what we can have and we are suffering terribly because of that. So I write another letter, because he refuses to have a conversation.

Sunday, June 25
"As I never have a chance to talk to you, I have decided to write a couple of words. I know that you do not like it when I praise you or thank you and that it does not flatter you at all, but I would like to express the gratitude I feel from the bottom of my soul. You are our God on earth, our benefactor and saviour, and we have seen proof of that on so many occasions; there were so many moments when one had to have doubts, but you have heroically adhered to your sacrifice. One does not know how much one can bear. Sometimes it seems that one cannot carry on living but you have such a strong will, and a lot can still be done with good intentions. You have been so kind to us that you can believe me that we take in every bite with emotion and tears in our eyes. But we cannot show you our boundless gratitude with anything else but our empty words. If only we still had some money or valuables to be able to repay at least some of our debt of gratitude. But we can only offer you our own souls. We are entirely at your mercy and you can do with us whatever you will, but you are humane and you know that we are living creatures and what we need most to survive. You have often said that every living creature you are taking care of will never come to harm. Why, we might succeed in this effort and then everything will prove worth your while. We are so happy that we can go out earlier, because it is like a second life to us. I understand what obligations you have toward the entire household, but you still show us such mercy, acting entirely according to Christ's principles, which oblige one to save his neighbour in need. In silent despair, we pray to God for you to continue taking care of us and to not let us perish, for us to remain strong enough to somehow survive until the end. I hope that God will listen to our pleas and reward us for our suffering."

The next day that Rascal came over and told us that we could only expect bread and water because all the food had run out. We could not accept that, because the hunger, or malnutrition, of the last couple of days had left us extremely exhausted.

Consequently, Kitten wrote another letter:
"My Dearest People! Have scruples, have mercy. Do not let us die of hunger. Do not refuse us your help. Do not change your attitude toward us. Death by starvation is horrible. I plead with you in the name of everything holy to continue saving us for our life depends on you. Let us stay for the summer and if the situation does not change we will give up. But do not let us starve during this time. I have nothing with which to pay you, so take the shoes, shirts and sweaters from us, even if it means stripping us naked, but do not let us starve, because this is the most crucial. Why, we do not demand any tidbits. The food can be [meatless?] *but let us eat our fill. Have mercy. Do not let us suffer so, because we are living creatures. Our hearts have become very weak. Jesus will reward you for this mercy. Do not let us die as long as the police do not find us. We are so poor and miserable. If we could go out we would go begging, but with the situation being as it is, we are entirely at your mercy...."*

And they began giving us beans. They are very good for [those who work?], *but not for us.*

July
That Rascal came to me on July 3 and on the 5th to Kitten. On the 10th to me again and on the 12th Kitten got angry and said she had to have some. She wrote a letter: "If you want me to, I will come late in the evening to the barn through the plank, because I cannot stand your lying alone so close under your eiderdown. I'm dying of desire for you because I have become possessed. I want to play with you for a moment, naked. I want to have all of you to myself. I am dying of lust. I need to have it as medicine. To hell with the war! Let us enjoy ourselves for a moment. You are my whole world. I will give it to you on the tip... Is it

going to get hard? For I become wet at the very thought. My love for you is so strong."

He came over, but he did not want to take Kitten to his place, so they did it at our place. But Kitten was glad anyway....

July 23, sex with me and on 25th with Kitten.
July 30, sex with Kitten from behind.

These days Ciuruniu is in a relatively good mood because of the assassination attempt and the approaching front.[23] *The day before yesterday he brought us four apples and today six. On the 30th Ciuruniu brought us a tiny bouquet of flowers. It can't be!!!*

Thursday, August 3
During the last couple of days the frontline moved much closer and now it is in the vicinity of Rzeszów.

Although August started relatively well for us, it soon got much more difficult. At first, we learned that the situation in the town was returning to normal. The worst thing is that the police have returned. Making matters worse, the frontline stopped and stuck near Radomyśl, just about a dozen kilometres from us.[24] *Ciuruniu has lost the spring in his step and was out of sorts.*

[August] *9 he stayed and had sex with me.*

---

23 A reference to the July 20, 1944, assassination attempt on Hitler.
24 In July 1944, the Soviet forces of the 1st Ukrainian Front under the command of Marshal Ivan Konev reached the borders of Dąbrowa Tarnowska county. And that is where they halted their advance — until the winter offensive, which started on January 12, 1945. Finally, the front stabilized along the Baranów-Radgoszcz-Jastrzabka line, leaving Dąbrowa Tarnowska still under the German occupation.

One Friday before bread baking, we were positively starving because we did not want to demand any food. And one beautiful Sunday, on the 27th, two elegant ladies visited our landlords. We were even happy that Ciuruniu and Madam would have some fun and we did not suspect that it would be the cause of a great part of our misery. After they left we found out that the ladies had a brother who was hiding to evade digging trenches and that they wanted him to be able to move in here and simply have room and board until something changed. And those naive people agreed and the very same day in the evening that bold barrel of fat rolled over with his bald head, all his bags and cases in front of him and behind him. They immediately found an eiderdown and a big pillow for him in fresh covers, while we, so miserable, must sleep on that one dirty throw pillow without a pillowcase. The very next day in the morning he examined the entire farm and peeked into our stable and caught a glimpse of me. But Ciuruniu and Madam convinced him that it must have been Emilia's son. Anyhow, we could not stay in the stable any longer and Ciuruniu moved us to the attic, where he made a cozy nest for us in the hay.

On the 29th he stayed with me for sex on the hay.

If it had not been for the heat we probably would have somehow endured, but the high temperature heats up the hay, which gives off a very harmful smell. We had a headache continuously day and night for two weeks. We lost our appetites so completely that all lunches were fed to the pigs. Kitten was the first to be taken sick, followed by me. We both had a fever, but it soon passed. When we had the fever we had to bite stale bread, because Ciuruniu had neglected us. They stuff all the food into 'his lordship's' mouth. It is so unfair that they take pity on him, even though he does not deserve it at all. For him they have bread with butter, with cheese, scrambled eggs and especially boiled milk with sugar, while we are given a small bottle of vodka and a bowl of tomatoes. Furthermore, we have not seen even one apple from the orchard and when I asked for a couple, Ciuruniu swiftly offered a lousy excuse, saying, "There are apples but they are hard and sour, so I don't know if you would like them."!!! He brought us some, neither hard nor particularly sour.

On September 2 I approached Ciuruniu and he stayed [with me].

Ciuruniu began to change again some time ago and he has been totally neglecting us. At first, he stopped calling on us in the evenings. But he still brought us some relatively good food three times a day, though he went days without saying a word to us. Well, tough luck. Then on September 9 the [German] troops arrived to be billeted here. And that was when he abandoned us completely. He has an excuse at hand that he cannot [take care of us], because the soldiers are staying in his home, but I do not believe that. 'His lordship' is the only obstacle, as the landlords devote all their thoughts to him, even though he does not need that at all. They will not eat anything, but they will stuff him, while feeding us is out of the question. They have completely forgotten about us. But when his sisters come over, they present them with whole bags of fruit, which surprisingly are neither hard nor sour, and with cheese and milk; the sisters also make cheesecakes, poppy seed cakes and so on, from the produce. By contrast, we, who need this milk and cheese to live and not for taste, see nothing else but stale bread for days on end. They sometimes throw us some tomatoes, because they are already rotting and everybody throws them at each other. When they cook lunch, then we have some potatoes at night. Every so often when they have something else they dispose of it, for how could they [bring it to us?] in the dark? And 'his lordship' is the only obstacle, not the soldiers, because he sticks his nose everywhere. This ape walks in the garden, enjoys the fresh air, has good food on time, eats his fill of apples, but he must be feeling worse than we are because he is still complaining. He is an exceptional coward and they take such pity on him. We, however, who have been sitting in a hole, continuously, for weeks since his arrival, without air, in the stench of pigs and hay dust, are not checked on even once during the day. What's more, Ciuruniu has even ceased to bring us water. They only throw in a pot with some food once a day, without so much as a word.

And today we do not even have bread. Madam only threw us three scraps. All this is because of the change that Rascal has undergone. He's thinking about 'his lordship' instead of about us.

On September 22 I approached Ciuruniu and asked him not to ignore us.

September. The entire month of September was awful.

Nothing new happened in October, but it was enough anyway. Though actually, there were many new developments, because we are receiving less food and it is bad and late. We are faring worse, in every respect. Ciuruniu has changed beyond recognition. He seems a different man. His behaviour has undergone a major change. We are awfully miserable because of that. November was another totally miserable month. On November 11 about a dozen Jews were escorted to Dąbrowa.[25] And on Monday, November 13, Tosiek [Antoni, one of Emilia's sons] *was severely wounded in both legs and he is in the hospital. But the danger to his life passed after a couple of days. On November 22, Ciuruniu came and said, [*"]Emilka[26] *does not want to bother with you anymore. I do not know what to do with you![*"] *How are we bothering Emilka? Is it that instead of bringing a pot of potatoes to the pigs she has to throw it into the hay in the attic? She's changed so much and she's treating us so cruelly. And how can Ciuruniu let us suffer so terribly?*

---

25 Melania makes reference to a massive manhunt for Jews that took place in the nearby Dulcza forest, during which a score of Jews were caught and many others were killed on the spot. The Jewish captives were later transferred to Auschwitz, Bergen-Belsen and other camps. Some of them survived the war.

26 Diminutive for Ciuruniu's sister.

December 1 began with sex with Kitten. And on December 5 she had sex some more. And on December [date missing] Ciuruniu came over at dawn and said that he had to go up to the frontline for ten days to dig trenches. And he left right away on the same day. That was when we learned what real misery was. As if we had not had enough of it already! Madam would come in the morning with watery milk and then late in the evening [we would receive] some scraps from the army soup. And we are never sure whether she will forget us, and if she will come. We are often so weak that we have no strength to go out onto the surface and beg Madam to continue sheltering us and not to abandon us, because otherwise we will certainly die a horrible death. I begged her to let us stay at least until Ciuruniu's arrival. I told her that Kitten was very weak and I begged her and kissed her hands to convince her to send at least one portion of something relatively nourishing for her. But that did not work either. Nothing can move her. She will not change her attitude toward us. She has become sick and tired of us and she hates us. We do not need her love but we are suffering because it is almost impossible for us to live in such conditions. If this doesn't change soon, we will not survive.

Ciuruniu came over the day before Christmas. We were so happy at the prospect of Christmas Eve and eating the seven dishes,[27] for we expected nothing else, particularly with Ciuruniu at home. But to our deep disappointment we were given thin army soup. And that thin soup cost us much of our health. So had they abandoned us to such an extent that we had Michalina's [the German cook] thin soup from all the dishes they prepared? Ciuruniu left for another two days to dig trenches and it seemed to us that our situation would surely improve after his return. He returned on New Year's Eve. At the beginning of the New Year the soldiers kept firing for half an hour and we were very scared that they

---

27 It is a tradition in Poland to serve an uneven number of dishes on Christmas Eve.

would hit the roof, because they were drunk. That Rascal finally came over in the morning with a bottle of vodka. Kitten asked him to take care of us so that we could somehow survive, and he told us that it was not worth our and their suffering, that it would fail anyway, that we would not survive, that he regretted that sacrifice and so on. We had nothing to say to those words of his. And it was so until the memorable Sunday of January 14 [1945]. At the break of dawn Ciuruniu comes over and says, ["L]isten to what I have to tell you: one lady has just come over and said that all men aged fourteen to sixty have to report for work on the other bank of the Dunajec River and that Dąbrowa will be evacuated by 2:00 p.m. So what should I do with you? I will hide with 'his lordship' in the barn but what should I do with you? People are saying that they shall be looking in nooks and crannies, because few men will have reported for work. So there is no other option; the only thing I can do is to cover you up with hay so thoroughly that you shall be barely able to breathe. And you need to survive on what you have.["] As we had nothing, Kitten asked him to bring us something, and he did throw us some food. He covered us in hay and left. We did not count on survival. We planned that when we saw the neighbours leaving we would leave, too, through the pigsty. I sewed a skirt from a blanket for Kitten and we waited, terribly anxious, to see what would happen. In the meantime we saw the soldiers pack up and leave. We thought how wonderful it would have been if it had not been for the fact that we were inside and that it was almost impossible for us to survive.

Later in the evening Ciuruniu came over and said that the [German] soldiers had left for Żabno, having taken the horse and a cow. We could hear explosions and blasts all night long. In the morning that Rascal came over and said that it was quiet and that there had been no major changes. Kitten was weak so she decided to beg Ciuruniu to save us because of our being very weak. When Ciuruniu heard her begging he lost his temper. He said hateful words, which we had never before heard from him. He said that he had no intention to continue helping us and *that he had already done too much, that he regretted all that and that none of it was worth his while. He began to reproach us for having excessive needs and for being so hungry despite having so much food the day before. He said, [*"*]Bugger off![*"*] and he was about to leave but Kitten stopped him by force and said, [*"*]I swear to God that if nothing changes within a week, that is by Monday, we will go out on our own, but do feed us for this week, so that we have strength to go out.[*"*] And he left. After a moment he brought us some soup. We had never felt more resigned. The night was deathly silent. We debated what to do after that week elapsed. For what might have changed there during six days, considering that six years had not done a thing. I convinced Kitten to tell that Rascal that I was pregnant, so that he would perhaps take pity on me and stop being so cruel. The aircraft were circling as usual, but we were not even afraid because we simply did not care anymore. Then Ciuruniu comes over and says, [*"*]You can be calm now, because there is no trace of the Germans. They have all left, blown up the bridges and burned down the [railway] station.[*"*] So that was how we were liberated from hell and we regained the freedom we had yearned for!!!*

co wypada nam uczynić po upływie tego tygodni
bo cóż się tu może zmienić przez 6 dni, jak 6 lat
nie nic zrobiły. Ja namówiłam kotuśkę, żeby
powiedziała kuncwolowi, że jestem w ciąży, to
może będzie miał litość nademną i nie będzie
taki okrutny. Samoloty krążyły jak zwykle, ale
nie baliśmy się, bo było nam wszystko jedno.
Wtem przychodzi ciuruniu i mówi: teraz już m
żecie być spokojniejsze, bo Niemców już ani śladu
niema, bo wszystko zwiało, mosty wysadzone,
a stacja spalona. W ten sposób więc przyszło-
wyzwolenie z piekła i wymarzona wolność !!!

The last page of Molly's diary. January, 1945.

Part Two: Molly's memoir

The woods are lovely, dark and deep,
But I have promises to keep,
And miles to go before I sleep,
And miles to go before I sleep.

— Robert Frost, "Stopping by Woods on a Snowy Evening" (1923)

In memory of my family and Victor and Emilia

Author's Preface

My life was shaped by the Holocaust. None of us know how long our memories will remain clear and vivid enough to evaluate thoughtfully. It is not a good idea to let time pass until it is too late to complete the project of writing a memoir. It is not for us to know how many years we will be granted, and I wrote this memoir because I don't want to have regrets that I neglected something that I consider of value.

I have come to the conclusion that what is most important in our lives is the family we leave behind — our genes and, even more so, our good name. It is priceless and cannot be changed or bought. Had we done wrong or acted with impropriety in the past, our name cannot be erased even if later we want to make restitutions. It is as if our names are written in stone. And most probably our pasts are passed on to the next generation — a burden even though they had nothing to do with them. (The sins of the fathers are visited upon the children.) Personally, I feel I have nothing to feel ashamed of, but I do wish I had given my children and grandchildren more attention.

I was selfish enough to go away down south for months at a time and mostly only had telephone contact. On the positive side, I was always there when financial need arose and was generous within my means. I also had the pleasure of making weekly Friday night dinners so that the children and grandchildren could get together. What

I wish to witness before I am gone is to see that my children make a decent living and don't struggle so hard. It would make me feel that they are not waiting for an inheritance, of which little may be left. It is my belief that money earned is highly valued, but money given or inherited is easily spent, since it was not worked for by the sweat of the brow.

Later in my life I developed a hobby of sewing Barbie doll clothes, which gave me great pleasure, sewing them or giving them away. I started a little too late for my granddaughters to play with, but they always admired my efforts and said they were awed by my work. My collection will eventually belong to them, as part of my legacy, and perhaps some as-yet-unborn great-grandchildren will play with them and be told who made them.

I regret at this late date that my grandchildren will know about me only that I came from Poland, survived the Holocaust, came to Canada, made many dinners and sewed Barbie clothes. I did not spend enough time with them when they were little and would have willingly listened to the stories of my survival, early life and struggles in Canada. Alas, it is too late. I get respect from them, an occasional short visit or telephone call, and that's all. This is just the way life is. They have either work or school or both, and their own interests and friends, and there just is not enough time for everything.

History repeats itself. I did not make enough time for my own children, even though their needs were looked after. In retrospect, we made some good decisions. Our family took trips to Israel and other European countries, which left many pleasant memories. However, I feel that their emotional needs were not met. We did not tell them we loved them or that we were proud of them and they were treasured. Because we never got this type of affection in our own lives growing up, I had no example to follow and did not see the need.

When my children were young, neither I nor my husband, Rubin, talked about the Holocaust. I wish I knew why not. There were plenty of opportunities. When one of the children asked their father what the meaning was of the tattooed number on his arm, he told them that it was to remember his phone number. It was such an opportune moment to give them age-appropriate information and then continue as they were growing up. Once, the children asked me why they didn't have grandparents and I made the explanation short, saying that they had all been killed by the Germans during the war.

I now realize what little part religion played in our lives. Candles were lit Friday nights, we attended synagogue on the High Holidays and the children were sent for Jewish education to after-school classes. We attended various simchas but it seems that God never came under discussion. I do not know what my children's beliefs in God are. I wonder if it is too late to ask. In the future, they and their families might read my autobiography and learn more about my past and Judaism. It will be up to them. I have done my part and put it all on paper to the best of my ability. The rest is in their hands.[1]

---

1 Molly wrote her memoir between 1998 and 2001.

The Market Square

Life in Poland was always tough, especially for Jews, and even more so for Orthodox Jews. They were ostracized, ridiculed and picked on; their different clothes and haircuts were made fun of. The Polish population was predominantly Catholic, and it was not that they hated Jews — apparently they just did not like the looks of their different clothes, haircuts and customs, and the fact that they kept to themselves. The Poles were also taught in church that Catholicism was the only true religion.

The government was not sympathetic. But what were the Jews to do? Some managed to buy a passage to the New World, but for the majority it was impossible to save up enough for a ticket, so unless they had help from abroad, they just carried on. Sometimes, enough was saved up for the price of one ticket, and then usually the head of the family was dispatched, with the idea of saving up, in time, to bring the rest of his family to join him. Wives and children were left behind to wait, sometimes for years. America's streets were not paved with gold after all, and the new arrivals struggled to find work and learn the language.

I recall glimpses of the hatred that was embedded in some of the Polish gentiles. My parents had a store in Krakow and we sold fruit, candy, beer, sandwiches, soda and such. We lived in the back of the store, which was in an area where most of the hospitals were located, and when people came to visit patients, they'd buy an orange, grapes or candy to bring to the patients, or refreshments for themselves after travelling some distance. The store brought in a good living, but saving was next to impossible. Many times we'd get up in the morning and find some of the signboards on our store defaced with paint. The messages read, "Do not buy from Jews"; "Jews, go to Palestine"; or "We urge you to buy from your own." We would then hire a teenager, the son of the superintendent, to clean it up — for a price, of course — and it was our suspicion that it was he, perhaps with a friend, who had done it in the first place. But that was the way it was, until the next time. When one of my brother's playmates taunted him, saying, "Jew boy, Jew boy," he'd retaliate with, "Yes, I am a Jew, but my family has a store, and your family has nothing."

Before the war, my mother, Sara, was widowed when my father, Fivel, died suddenly. I think he must have had a heart attack. I have a mental picture of him walking to the hospital across the street and then, a few hours or a day later, my mother coming home and throwing his hat on the bed, crying, then relatives or friends coming to the apartment. A lot of candles were burning in the next room. Nothing was said to me of what was happening, then or later. After a time — I must have been around six years old — my playmates taunted me, saying that my father was dead, but I denied it and then went to ask my mother. She told me that my father had gone away to the countryside for fresh air; I guess that's the way death was dealt with in those times, everything hush hush. My mother was stuck running the store and taking care of two very young children, one an infant. Though she was one of ten siblings and had a mother, I don't believe anyone came to help. After approximately two years, she remarried to an older bachelor named Ignac, and this was also done in secret from us children. We were not informed that a new father was going to be living with us. I recall a man coming to the store and talking to my mother, and her preparing some food for him. I don't remember him ever being introduced to me or paying me any attention then or later. It felt like I was just being tolerated.

After some time passed, I figured it out on my own. One summer, shortly before the war, I was sent to a summer camp, and we were told to write letters home. My letters were always titled, "Dear Mommy." One day, my mother wrote that the next letter I wrote should read, "Dear parents." I suppose my feelings were best expressed in just these two words. I don't know how I remember this so vividly. Much later in my life, I was taking some night courses at Seneca College and one course was Psychology 101. One of the lectures was on death and dying, and of trying to recall our first experience with death. That's when these memories surfaced. I think it is generally believed now that no matter how painful things are, it's better to disclose them and deal with them in the open.

On September 1, 1939, when I was almost nine years old, war broke out in Poland. The German army overran Poland in about three weeks. There was some bombing and the cellars became bomb shelters, but Krakow was a historic city and the Germans did not want to destroy it, so not much damage was done. The persecution against Jews started very slowly in Krakow. At first, every family was issued a ration card and the Jews got a slightly smaller ration. A few months later, the Germans told us to move; we had to give up our store and apartment, and the Jewish committee helped us find a place to live in the rundown Jewish section of the city. There was no way to make a living any longer; I guess we lived off our savings. It was getting harder and harder to buy extra food on the black market, and the rations were quite insufficient.

When the war broke out, we already knew that the Germans hated the Jews, but the consensus among most people was that only men were in danger because surely the Germans would not do anything to women and children. Many families decided that the best option was for men to cross the Soviet border, which was wide, with forests and rivers, and apparently not too hard to cross. In my family, my uncle Josef, who was married to my mother's sister Frania, decided to flee to the Soviet Union. And so it was that his wife, Frania, and their two children, Janus (Jacob) and Krysia (Kreindel), were left behind. Frania suggested we come and live with her and her mother-in-law, Shaindel, in the town of Dąbrowa Tarnowska, which was just over one hundred kilometres away. At some point in 1940, we took Frania up on her offer, left Krakow with all our belongings, furniture and all, and travelled to Dąbrowa.

Josef had a little photography studio, which was vacant, and so my mother, my stepfather, Ignac, my little brother, Zygmunt (Zyga) and I moved into the studio and got a small simple wooden stove. In the meantime, living and surviving in Krakow was getting tougher and tougher so my aunt Antosia, her husband, Max, their two children, Ala and Shlomo, and my cousin Helen also came to Dąbrowa. They moved in with Frania, into her one room and kitchen. It was quite crowded, but after all, they were family, it was wartime, and survival was the only important project. The studio I lived in with my family was right across the marketplace, so close to my cousins, and we children got together almost daily to play. Since we were not allowed to attend school, Antosia's daughter, Ala, and I were trying to teach the younger children a little reading.

My uncle Adolf (Abe), my mother's brother, who was the youngest of the ten siblings, also lived in the same tenement building as our other cousins. His family — his wife, Rozia, and their smart little three-year-old boy, Alfred — had left Krakow as well. I knew Uncle Adolf better than my other relatives because he had spent more time with me. When he used to visit us in Krakow with my grandmother Pearl, they stayed with us, and what stuck in my memory was how he looked after his mother, who was elderly and not well. She suffered from diabetes, and her legs were full of varicose veins. My grandmother wore high-laced shoes, and he would help her put them on and lace them up. Little gestures like that stay in a child's memory.

It was a little easier to get food supplies in the shtetl than it had been in Krakow. Dąbrowa was surrounded by countryside, and the villagers would come twice a week to the market, bringing their wares to sell or barter. Mostly, it was bartering for goods, because money had little value. My mother sold our possessions — linens, some dishes, clothes, whatever was available and in demand — in exchange for food.

We lived a simple life. In the middle of the market square were water pumps and everyone in town came there to get water. For whoever could afford it, there were water carriers for hire; they carried two pails on a sling on their shoulders and the water was deposited into a wooden barrel, which every household had. Everything was primitive — a few families shared an outdoor toilet and washing facilities were practically non-existent, as was soap — but as I remember it, we managed, and I was not bothered by our new situation at all. I had my cousins whom I liked very, very much, and I was surrounded by Jewish customs and speech. On a Friday afternoon it was my job to take a pot with vegetables or a piece of meat thrown in, a stew called cholent, to the baker. Most everyone in the shtetl did this. Everyone marked their names on top of the pot, and on Shabbat I went again to the baker, armed with a towel to carry it back home. The baker called out people's names as he pulled the pots out of the oven. I collected our cholent, which was so hot that I could smell it as I marched home. Whatever was inside always tasted delicious and satisfied our hunger. A portion of cholent was enough for the rest of the day.

It was in Dąbrowa that I first picked up a smattering of the Jewish language and customs. My little brother, Zyga, was quite taken by it all, and started doing the prescribed Jewish rituals. I remember the hand washing before first speaking in the morning; Zyga prepared a glass of water close to his bed because he told me that he was allowed to take only three steps before washing his hands. He was also learning to daven, or pray, and there were plenty of neighbours willing to help.

When winter came, I had no shoes that fit me anymore; I had outgrown mine and they were given to one of the younger cousins. My mother managed to get me a pair of galoshes from someone, and that was it. No shoes were available. But I was young, and beside the fact that my toes got frostbitten that winter (there were no socks either) and as long as I was not too hungry, it was all right with me.

But things were getting worse. There were random beatings and shootings, apparently for those who had supposedly broken some rules. One evening, in the spring of 1942, a few German policemen came into the tenement building where our cousins, including Helen, lived. They were searching for a Jew who had not shown up for forced labour that morning, and they could not locate him. They banged on doors and stormed into apartments in the building until they entered our cousins' two-room apartment. I was there when they decided to take my uncle Max, saying they would question him at their head-quarters. He was the only man in that family, as the rest were women and children — Frania; her two children, Janus and Krysia; Antosia, Max's wife; their two children, Ala and Shlomo; and Helen and her mother, Shaindel.

The Germans did not take Max for questioning. They took him into the marketplace a few steps away from the building and shot him dead in full view. He was the first victim in our family, and we were all in a state of shock, having seen this senseless murder with our own eyes. I can still see in my mind's eye the pool of blood after his body was removed. Our relatives' windows faced the marketplace, and some kind Christian neighbour realized this and brought a couple of pails of sand to cover up the puddle of blood. The family sat a proper shiva and mourned. Antosia sat in the corner for a few days as if paralyzed. Since Max was my mother's brother, she also sat shiva.

The struggle for food and, therefore, survival went on. Soon a command appeared that was posted everywhere: all Jews had to surrender their jewellery and furs over one foot long, under threat of death for not complying. People started turning in some of their valuables, hiding the rest or giving them for safekeeping to their gentile friends. Some tried to avoid turning in their fur coats, resorting to cutting them up and making them into slippers.

Next came the collection of good furniture. When the transport trucks arrived, the German police went through people's homes, inspected their goods and just simply took away the furniture they deemed suitable. They were quite choosy — there was a lot to choose from — and the Jewish labour force was not immune to this order. If their furniture was judged suitable, the Germans hauled it away as well. Our furniture, too, was taken away. My mother scribbled our family name inside our kitchen credenza, perhaps hoping to get it back some day. It probably ended up in Germany.

I visited my cousins daily, and that day, I found them lying on mattresses on the floor. The furniture had been taken. The younger children did not take this very seriously and they were jumping on the mattresses, as children will. I guess they did not see it as such a calamity. Photos and clothes and other items from the now non-existent drawers floated to the floor or in the corners of the room, and we children just rummaged through them. Many family mementoes were sitting in piles in the corner, being ignored by the adults who had bigger concerns for the day, mostly how to go about getting some additional food to supplement the bread rations. A package of letters tied with a ribbon surfaced; they happened to be letters that my uncle Adolf had written to his prospective bride. One letter read, "If you marry me, I will be a good husband to you and a good father to our future children, as I am now a good son and brother." Even though we called Adolf and Rozia "Pat and Patachon" behind their backs, after a comical duo whose funny height difference matched theirs, they were a well-matched pair in other ways.

After the furniture order, a strange command followed: Anyone whose windows were facing the market square was ordered to have flower boxes made to fit the windows, and geraniums or petunias had to be planted. I recall my aunt Frania saying, "Here I am, no means to buy food, and yet I have to have window boxes made and flowers planted. How ironic."

But, we carried on, mostly concerned with getting enough food to survive another day. All of us children were so well trained that no one stole any food. We just waited until a piece of bread was cut for us or we were given whatever else was available, which was mostly vegetables like rutabagas, carrots, potatoes or radishes.

We eagerly searched for news about the war but heard nothing. In those years very few people had radios, and those who did had had to turn them in to the authorities long before. It was forbidden to listen to the radio, should anyone still own one illegally. The newspaper printed only censored news; we were completely cut off from the rest of the world. We were forbidden, under threat of death, to leave or travel beyond the borders of the town. Later, this was restricted even more, to just a small corner of the town. The only news that reached us was the fact that Germany had broken the non-aggression pact with the Soviet Union in June 1941 and had declared war on the country. Otherwise, we lived in a vacuum, concerned only with surviving each day.

I handled the everyday stress my own way. A young girl a few years older than I had befriended me. Sabina Goldman worked in her father's shoe store right below my cousins' apartment. She was wise beyond her years. She had grown up in Dąbrowa, and her family was better off than ours. She'd slip me an apple or some other goodie from time to time, and I grew to like her a lot. In time, I practically worshipped her. I hung on her every word.

There was not much for sale in the shoe store and then only on ration cards, but the German authorities insisted that all the stores be kept open anyway. So Sabina took over her father's job and came every morning to open the store. I would rush to my cousins' apartment early in the morning just to get a glimpse of her coming to open the store and see her wave to me. Sometimes she'd invite me to her parents' apartment for dinner and a sleepover, and I lived for those times. I tried to memorize every detail of the visit, her clothes and her every word. When she decided she'd teach me a few words of English,

I was very eager. Perhaps she was giving me the attention I was not getting at home.

Sabina volunteered in the soup kitchen, where one meal of soup was provided from time to time. The work required that several people stay and guard the pot so that no one stole from it; people were so hungry that they couldn't wait for the distribution, and they'd come with a pail, dip it into the huge cauldron and run away. I witnessed this because I searched out the places where I knew Sabina would be. I wanted to be near her. Sabina was usually surrounded by friends and I watched them from a distance, but I was not asked to join them.

~

New proclamations were posted almost daily, which had to be followed to the letter, or else. Teenage boys and young men were to report for forced labour or were simply picked off the streets and made to work at menial or back-breaking jobs. Since we were so insulated, we didn't know if this was happening everywhere or just where we were. Some of the young men were forced to dig up the headstones in the cemetery and then lay them as sidewalks, especially in our area of town. The Hebrew inscriptions had to be facing up, as an extra bit of cruelty.

Helen found herself a job as a gardener at the German headquarters, tending flower beds and doing other such tasks. No one else in the family had a job; they were near impossible to get. It was generally felt that it was good to hold an important job, as people who worked might not be bothered and might also be assigned a bigger food ration.

At that time, the grownups in the family decided that we should hide some of our remaining more valuable possessions. A few wooden floorboards were dug up in the studio, and the family all got together and placed under the boards some candlesticks, silverware, wine cups, the head of a sewing machine, tablecloths and even some clothes. Some of the jewellery that had not yet been sold or exchanged for food was also gathered and hidden somewhere in the studio. That secret place was not shown to us kids, but I knew about the floorboards. I wasn't aware, then, that the little building where the studio was located belonged to our family. I don't know whose name it was in, but I found out after the war that it used to belong to my maternal grandmother, Pearl.

Above the studio was an attic, and the people who lived in the other little buildings in our courtyard shared the space for drying clothes. Together, they partitioned off a small corner of the attic and put in a very tiny camouflaged door, where men could possibly hide in case we heard rumours that the Germans were rounding up men for labour or to take as hostages. Rumours were the only source of information, true or not.

It was around this hectic time, the spring of 1942, that I began writing in a diary, confiding my thoughts and fears.

The Last Witness

I am the last witness to this part of the family saga. It happened so many years ago, and yet many facts and details are branded into my brain.

Early one morning in June 1942, we heard a lot of strange noises and then shooting and more shooting. Not knowing what it was about, my family and the neighbours in our courtyard decided to gather in our hiding place in the attic. The shooting, yelling and screams went on most of the day. We stayed there, shivering with fear and worrying should anyone sneeze or cough. I think people were ready to strangle each other if anyone made some noise. It felt like a fight to stay alive.

In the evening, when the noises had stopped, someone ventured out to assess the situation. It was then that we found out that a lot of trucks had appeared in the marketplace and that the German police had chased hundreds of Jews out of their homes, into the marketplace. They had shouted, "Raus! Raus!" (Out! Out!) and did not allow anyone to take anything with them. Our entire family — Shaindel, Antosia, Helen, Frania and the four children — was taken. It had been early morning and the children were not quite dressed for the day; little Krysia, who was about six years old, did not have her shoes on and was not allowed to put them on, and so, barefoot, she went with the others to the marketplace.

There were unbelievable cries and noises; no one knew what was happening. The German police started to force people into covered trucks, and as soon as the truck was overloaded, it left. Helen happened to have with her the piece of paper stating that she was employed by the German headquarters. It was her most treasured possession. She showed it to one of the Germans and he told her to just go, get away from there. She was allowed to leave, still waving that piece of paper, and she had gone straight to her job. That evening, we found out that she was the only one left from our family. She had no one else, just us. She stayed in the now-empty apartment for a little while and then gathered whatever of value was still left, abandoned the apartment and came to stay with us. Helen was now part of our little family.

The whole town was in shock. There was total bedlam. The trucks were gone, but people were walking around just stunned, not knowing what to do next. We were now living permanently on guard. Most everyone was sleeping fully dressed, just in case, because so many had witnessed others being taken away practically undressed, barefoot. No one would reveal where they had a hiding place; they kept it to themselves.

Another phenomenon was taking place. The remaining people were looting the empty homes in search of leftover food and ration cards. Helen located some abandoned ration cards, and for a while we had the extra bread.

It felt as though life was on automatic. We heard rumours that all the missing people were taken to the East, to work on farms, but we wondered how they could survive without clothes, shoes and other basics. I think we preferred to be deceived; the truth would have been too harsh to swallow. We didn't find out until much later that this was the first transport from Dąbrowa to the death camp of Bełżec.

~

That summer, my mother befriended a farmer, Victor, and his sister, Emilia. She asked them to consider giving us some work on the farm in exchange for a meal — as I mentioned, jobs were impossible to get. We went to the city hall with them and received a permit to work on the farm. This would allow us to leave the border of the town during the daytime, but we were under orders to be back before dark. We spent the next few weeks going to the farm; it was harvest time, and we were put to work harvesting beans and beets and weeding rows of potatoes. On some days we worked quite late. It was easier to be in the fields when it was not so hot anymore, and on these occasions we were encouraged to sleep over in the barn, despite our permit orders. This way, we were ready for work early the next morning.

Emilia was a widow; her husband had died suddenly just before the war. She had three young children — Zdzisław, Antoni and Barbara — who were all under seven years of age. When her husband died, she struggled on the farm because there was no money to hire someone to help out. She was going under. Victor, on the other hand, was a bachelor living and working on his parents' farm in another village. Having a good heart, he decided to come to his sister's aid until she managed to sort herself out somehow. A few months later the war broke out, and he stayed on and took over the task of running the farm. Without him, she would have been lost on that tiny farm. There was just one horse and two cows, some chickens, a pig or two, a dog. It was a poor farm. But Victor was resourceful. He planted a lot of onions, and when they were ripening and ready for harvesting, he slept in the onion patch to protect it from night thieves. He also built a little glass cage, like a solarium, and sowed some tomato seeds early in the spring so that the plantings were ready for the fields earlier than anyone else's. He planted rows of tomatoes, not just the red ones but other varieties, and when they ripened, the tomatoes were taken to the market and were a good early cash crop along with the onions. This was easier and cheaper than making and selling cheese and butter from the two cows.

At the end of June, yet another proclamation was posted; this one gave us a few weeks to move into a concentrated, rundown part of town, a precursor to a ghetto. My mother kept asking people to take us in, but everyone was so crowded as it was, and they probably preferred to make room for people they knew. We were, after all, strangers. I guess my mind was still that of a child's — at almost twelve years old I was not so much worried as curious about where we would wind up that night.

Finally, on the last day before we had to move, a family with one teenage boy, who lived in one room, took pity and decided to let us come and stay on their enclosed front porch. Our few remaining possessions were piled up in one corner and my mother set up a place to sleep on the floor for me and my brother. It was dusk, mid-July, and the days were long. A local Polish man walked by, an acquaintance of my mother's, and told us that he had just come from the area of the train station, where Jews were forbidden to go. He said that he had seen a lot of empty cattle wagons there. That was quite unusual for a little town like Dąbrowa. I guess my parents knew that this was a bad sign and suspected what was about to happen. We got dressed and walked across the square, one at a time so as not to attract attention, and snuck back to our previous hiding place in the attic. Some of our former neighbours also joined us. This was now the forbidden area. Around us were the empty little houses that had been so full of life just that morning. I think there was a pail to be used as a toilet. I do not recall if there was any water. We sat on the attic floor, not knowing what to expect.

It was before dawn when we heard the first shouts as the police entered our empty homes. I will never forget the sound of their boots breaking down the doors and the shouting and swearing; they sounded drunk and surprised that no one was there. The places really looked abandoned — no furniture, no possessions — so they went on to rampage across the square, where we had been only hours before. They did not bother to search our attic. Some people were holding their hands against others' mouths to prevent them from making any sound. We heard later that many babies were smothered that night by their parents in hiding. All that day we heard screams and gunfire. It wasn't until sundown that one of us ventured out; the rest waited until dark to cross the square and then we returned to our previous place on the porch.

People were already collecting corpses. Some people had been shot, some trampled to death — many small children had been squashed underfoot in the panicked crowd. Blood puddles were everywhere. In the midst of it, someone was setting up a fire to make an outdoor kitchen, trying to feed the confused, shocked people who had been left behind. Families had been separated and young children wandered here and there, looking for their parents — alas, in vain. Some kind soul would collect them and lead them away.

Though the burial society was no longer in existence, somehow the bodies were collected and buried in a mass grave. A large portion of town was now cleared of the Jewish population. I suppose the Nazis took only as many as would fit in the cattle wagons. I learned much later that on that day, July 17, about 1,800 Jews were deported to Bełżec.

When we returned to the place on the porch, we discovered that the couple who had taken us in the night before, and their teenage son, were gone. We now had the place to ourselves. All their belongings had been left behind, of course. Victor and Emilia delivered some food to us and in exchange we gave them clothes and household goods, since we now had plenty. We searched for the couple's ration cards and used them, as well as some of the food that they had squirreled away. We still could not comprehend what was happening, but we knew instinctively that it was better not to be caught and shipped away. I only knew I was scared, and I missed my cousins.

One day Victor said to us, "If it gets very scary in town again, run away to us." There was no discussion about the length of time, or where he would shelter us, or any other logistics of this proposal. It was just a sentence, said.

A few weeks later, the rumours started again about another raid coming up. We stayed that night on the farm, but it was quiet in the town, and after another couple of days we returned. The rumours were sometimes just that, rumours.

That September, everyone felt something big was coming. We were observing carefully what was going on around us and drew our conclusions from this, right or wrong. The Jewish police were under orders from the Germans to make sure that no Jewish family remained living in the forbidden part of town. When they did find someone and delivered them to the SS, they received an award of extra rations for their own families. Occasionally, we heard that they turned in members of their own extended families. It was a time of dog eat dog — the will to survive was so strong that it is not for us to judge them.

I still have a picture in my mind's eye of a couple of these Jewish policemen. People were envious of their position, believing that they had a better chance of staying alive. They strutted around in their special uniforms, armed with rubber batons that they were urged to use, whether necessary or not. They were ordinary men from our midst, but the situation lifted them up and I recall people saying that any of them could be bribed with valuables so as not to reveal if they found someone in the wrong part of town. One of the grownups said, "Even at this horrible time, a diamond still has some value even if nothing else does."

I thought I had long since erased all these details from my conscious memory, but now I find they come to the surface as I write this history. The brain records everything that we hear and see and stores the information, but it cannot be retrieved at will. However, it does come to the surface when there is a stimulus. I have not thought about some of these things for many, many years, and some of my memories only emerge as I go along recording the facts of approximately fifty-five years ago.

Then one day it happened. The Nazis decided to clear out the remainder of the Jews and make Dąbrowa *judenrein*, cleansed of Jews.

We decided to go into hiding on the farm, and we slept over in the barn when the last raid took place, taking almost everyone. Anyone left was spared only for the time being. I think people were resigned to their fate by that time.

Just before I went into hiding, I informed Sabina that I was going, and she held my head close to her chest and blessed me. I was crying, and she saw how distraught I was. We both had a feeling that we would never see each other again. She promised me that the next time she saw Victor or Emilia, she would write me a few words, which she did. I still have that short note to this day, more than fifty years later. It is dated September 11, 1942. Sabina was young, pretty and wise beyond her years. Here is the translated text of her letter:

My dear child, there is not much to write, and whatever I do write will be stupid, empty and banal, but you know I have no talent for writing. We have never been in such a situation before, and we are helpless. I do not believe running away or hiding will help any. Never! We have to accept our fate and talk ourselves into thinking that we are over seventy years old and we have to make room in this world for others, not for our children and grandchildren but for our worst enemies. I think the Germans are right when they say that if any Jew survives the war, every German will have to bow to him so low as to touch the ground. I want to believe that some of us will survive, and I urge you to try.

Alas, I cannot abandon my parents. Whatever fate happens to them will happen to me. Be brave, and pray that we will still have a chance to meet in this life. I will always remember your devotion.

Your true friend, Sabina

A few days later, however, she did leave her parents, and together with her sister, took a train, which was forbidden, to travel somewhere safer. Alas, they were discovered on the train, removed and put in the local jail. After I received Sabina's letter, I wrote in my diary, "How can one accept the thought that it is already our end, that we are seventy years old, despite being in our prime, despite being only twenty years old! If only we might see each other again!"

I still have a few snapshots of Sabina. I guarded them together with my family photos and promised myself that after the war I would have a room dedicated to her memory, with enlarged snapshots hanging on the wall. I even made a sketch of the room. In reality it was not feasible to accomplish, but it was always bright in my memory. As fate would have it, Sabina's father survived a death camp; his wife did not. Sabina's father later married his wife's sister, who had been married to his brother who did not survive. After the war, back in Dąbrowa, Sabina's father was telling me the story of his survival in the death camp, and how there was nothing to recover of his possessions after he returned to Dąbrowa. It pained him that he did not even have photographs of his family. And there I was, listening and taking this all in, but I did not divulge the fact that I was in possession of a few snapshots of Sabina and her sister. I can only think, now, that I was afraid I would be asked to give them up, and I was not prepared to take that chance. I have these photos to this day. I am not proud of that decision, but then I am not proud of many other decisions I made in my life, even when I was much older.

Only in Whispers

We were now stuck in the barn and could not work in the fields anymore. A neighbour couldn't be trusted to know about us, nor could Emilia's three children. It was a life-or-death situation. There were posters everywhere warning the gentile population that the punishment for hiding a Jew was death on the spot. In the case of farmers, the Germans would shoot the household and burn down the farm, including its animals, as a warning to others.

Victor and Emilia were torn as to what to do with all of us. They were both strong believers in God and righteousness. But after a few days in the barn, my stepfather decided that he could not bear to live this way — there was no water to wash with, and he had always been very careful about cleanliness — and instead would go back to town with Zyga to figure out what to do next. He instructed Victor to come to the house with a wagon, which Victor did, and they loaded up the wagon with children's clothes, utensils, pillows, comforters, a grinding machine and whatever else would fit. This was the rest of our family possessions; the other family's things were gone. At night, back on the farm, Victor and Emilia unloaded it all, hid some things and put to use some of the clothes and household goods.

A little later, my stepfather, Zyga and the remaining Jews were taken away by truck to the Tarnów ghetto, about twenty kilometres away, but Zyga managed to escape one day and return to us. Now only the Jewish police were left in town, still searching and gathering the left-over valuables. I was told later, when we were liberated, that the Polish population did little looting — it was strongly forbidden and the punishment was too severe to take a chance. However, they were allowed, after a time, to take over the now empty tenements.

It was on a frosty December 1942 morning that the news from town reached us: the Jewish police had been informed that their job was now finished and they, too, would be transported to the Tarnów ghetto. They were told to prepare for their departure together with their families. This information was obtained from the local townspeople who were witnesses to the whole procedure. At the appointed gathering spot, the Jewish police boarded the prepared trucks for the journey to Tarnów and said their goodbyes to Polish friends and acquaintances. They were driven instead to the Jewish cemetery, where they were forced to undress. All were shot. We heard that their clothes were just loaded with valuables. Some locals were selected to take apart every seam in the clothes under the watchful eyes and guns of the Nazis.

Our last scrap of hope was gone with them. We finally realized, and accepted, that no one was being resettled, that it had been a big lie to keep us unaware and hoping against hope and not believing what was incomprehensible to believe. We still did not know there would be mass destruction of Jewish populations and that it was happening all over Europe. Perhaps we would not have wanted to know at all.

My mother, Zyga, Helen and I were living in a corner of the barn, where Victor had built a lean-to. There was enough space for us to sit and lie down side by side. The shelter was covered by straw, with a little hidden exit. We sat there all day, and at night we crawled out and walked on the little barn floor, while listening for any noises around us. There was a doghouse nearby, and the dog was the early warning system of a stranger approaching. He was no protection from the children, but they were too young then to be running around late at night.

Through the cracks in the logs we were able to get glimpses of what was going on in the backyard, and often we watched the children playing and chasing each other or the chickens, the way kids do. My little brother was getting very restless; he could not sit all day in one tight spot, with nothing to do. He knew outside meant danger, but he wanted some freedom nevertheless. When we tried to explain to him why he could not go outside and play with the children, he wanted at least to go out at night and kick a ball around.

It was late December, and Victor and Emilia still had not decided what to do with us. They were hoping that the war would be over soon and that we would be able to leave the farm. In the meantime, many things were happening around us. Some Jews in hiding were betrayed by peasants, and instances were reported of farms and their inhabitants having been burned to the ground for hiding Jews. This kind of news spread like wildfire, of course, and even some determined Polish families were chasing the Jews they had been hiding out into the fields, where they could not survive long and perished, defeated by the elements, by hunger or by being reported to the German authorities.

One day, Victor told us that my little brother presented the biggest danger to us all and that he could not keep us any longer. Zyga had been constantly asking to go outside and play. Victor's sister, Emilia, and her three children were being endangered every day, and the children did not even realize how their lives were being affected. The children, of course, still had no idea that anyone was hidden on their farm. They had not seen us since the summer when we worked on the farm, but being children, they did not ask any questions. After all, workers come and go.

Negotiations, so to speak, went on, and my mother finally decided that she would try to travel to the Tarnów ghetto with my brother. Travel by any means of transportation was of course dangerous, but that was the only way. She dressed in the style of a peasant, with a kerchief tight around her head. It is possible that my mother felt that their departure might improve my and Helen's chances of staying alive. We had a heart-wrenching parting scene; we all realized it was doubtful we would ever see each other again.

I don't recall my brother's reactions or feelings; being a child, he was probably looking forward to once again being outside and not in this tight confinement, speaking only in whispers. My brother was blond and blue-eyed, so he didn't look like a stereotypical Jew. In the very early morning hours, Victor walked them to the railway station, a ticket was bought, and he waited until the train departed. A couple of weeks later we knew that they had reached the Tarnów ghetto because a postcard arrived from my mother. They had successfully sneaked into the ghetto, which was all cordoned off. They were there illegally, which meant without a ration card. I assume they survived for a while, but that was the last we heard of them.

Now just the two of us were left in the corner of the barn. Logistically, we now had a little more space, but we still clung to each other for comfort and for warmth. Victor and Emilia seemed a little more relaxed. The danger was the same, but with my brother gone, at least one threat of being discovered had been averted.

It was now January 1943. Victor must have had a gut feeling that the war was not going to end anytime soon, and there were no signs of an imminent end. Now he started to worry about our safety in the barn, as the straw was depleted. He decided that a better, and in his eyes a safer, site had to be found. He had an old wooden box that he enlarged a bit, and the finished product was approximately the size of a clothes wardrobe used widely in Poland. He then chose a place under the horse stable to bury that box.

Next, he and Emilia started digging the soil at night, removing the dirt and spreading it somewhere to conceal it. It took them several nights to dig out a hole big enough to accommodate the box. It was then buried, and a small opening was left for an entrance. I can only estimate the size of the box, but I remember it was just a few inches short for us to stretch our legs. The width was about that of a double bed, and the height not high enough for us to sit up; we could only lean on our elbows in a semi-sitting position. All day long we lay in that box, with just a tiny palm-sized hole for air to the outside. Only at night could we crawl out into the stable for our natural functions, to stretch our limbs and glimpse at the outside world through the cracks in the stable door.

Since we could not hold our pee all day, Victor brought us a hot water bottle (which had come with other items from our place in Dąbrowa) and an old rusty cooking pot. So, we peed into the pot and then transferred it to the hot water bottle, which we emptied at night in the horse stable. We had an old curtain that we used as a sheet to cover the straw we lay on. We also had one pillow, which we shared, and a feather-filled sort of comforter. I think it was called a feather-bed. It was popular in Europe, where there was no central heating and the pot-bellied stoves would cool off at night. We had only each other and the featherbed to keep us warm. As long as we were covered up, we were relatively warm. We also had a small jug, a knife and two spoons. And that was it. The jug held our precious water, the knife served for cutting bread, and the two spoons, which were never washed, were licked clean.

～

Emilia's cottage was similar to other cottages in the village, and probably to most village cottages in Poland at that time. The roof was covered with thatched straw and the cottage was built of logs and whitewashed. The living quarters consisted of one room only, with a dirt floor and an adjoining small room that was used as a pantry to hold grain, vegetables and clay pots of curdling milk waiting to be made into cheese or butter. There was a large stove in which bread was baked periodically and daily cooking was done, and that same stove heated the room. Sometimes, in the middle of the winter, the children slept near the stove to keep warm. Of furniture, there were two beds, a table with a couple of chairs and a bench that opened up into a bed. Emilia and young Barbara shared one bed; the two boys shared the other bed; and Victor slept on the bench. In one corner there was a foot-pedalled sewing machine. There was also a credenza where some dishes and cutlery were stored, and a barrel with clean water and a pail for dirty water. The other side of the cottage held the cow stable, the chicken coop and a small pigsty. All this was under the same roof. The outhouse was, of course, outside.

In the summer, one could hear the constant buzz of flies; they were everywhere, covering the walls and ceiling, falling into food while it was being consumed. From time to time the children would open the two small cottage windows and chase some of the flies out with tree branches. It was a losing battle. Only night and darkness brought some relief from their buzz. Emilia sometimes sewed at night by the light of a small oil lamp. Since oil was also rationed, they used it mostly in the darkness of winter. During winter, the family had a little more time because there was no field work, so Emilia would patch clothes or re-make some of the clothes that had come from our possessions. She had three growing children to dress somehow.

In the tiny entrance hall that separated the living quarters from the animal quarters, there was a millstone for converting grain like rye and wheat into flour. This was a tedious job, and Victor did it. The grain had to be thrown by handfuls into the middle of the millstone, which was kept spinning and turning to convert the grain into flour. Many nights we could hear, across the courtyard, Victor singing to himself while grinding the grain. Rye was used for making bread, and wheat, which was tastier and whiter, was made into noodles for Sunday dinners. Before dinner could be cooked, Emilia sent the two boys out with a sackcloth bag to collect twigs and loose branches for firewood. Since matches were in short supply, one of the boys would run to the neighbours and bring back a flame on a stick. It was wartime and there were shortages of everything.

The three children, Zdzisław, Antoni and Barbara, loved their uncle Victor. They were obedient to him as well as to their mother. During the entire time I spent on the farm, I did not hear any arguments. The children all had chores to attend to after school and did them cheerfully. They cleared the cow stable and put fresh bedding down for the cows. They fed the chickens and collected eggs. During the summer months, the children took the two cows out into the pasture to graze. With the warm weather, the cottage's windows were open and we heard the evening prayers being said; their young voices carried across the courtyard. This whole time, our presence had to be concealed from them. They could have unwittingly given away our being there to their playmates or neighbours, which would have spread to others and then brought on terrible danger to us and to them as well.

In the courtyard there was a well, a simple hole with wooden planks around it. A bucket was attached to a long wooden limb, and the water had to be drawn up hand over hand. This was mostly the grownups' job; though we observed the children trying on occasion, they were still too young for this chore. Having enough water was always a problem. It is clear in my memory how we suffered from thirst even more than from hunger. We were given a pitcher of water from time to time, but it was never enough. We tried to use some of the precious water for washing ourselves while in the stable, with just one mouthful of water.

Victor or Emilia brought us food sporadically. Emilia did not cook every day. She worked in the fields; three times a day she milked the cows; and she made cheese and butter, baked bread and hauled water. On Sundays after church she cooked a proper meal. The rest of the week it was just bread, cheese, eggs or whatever vegetable was available. On a Sunday, Victor would kill a chicken and Emilia would pluck it, cook it and make noodles. That was a treat, as we would then usually get a taste of it as well. Emilia also roasted soya beans to make ersatz coffee. Sometimes millet or barley was cooked for breakfast.

The delivery of food to us was quite complicated because it had to be concealed from the children, as they were not too young to notice when food was being placed in a basket and covered up with straw for the run to the stable. Another concern was that neither Emilia nor Victor be observed entering the stable too often, which would have been out of place and suspicious. One neighbour even asked Victor if he was hiding Jews. Victor vehemently denied it and then started leaving the stable door open during the daytime, which meant we could no longer get out during the day.

Before this incident with the neighbour, when things were quiet, which was usually in the winter, we would be allowed to venture out into the stable during the day. Then, one of us would stay by the shut door and look out into the courtyard through the cracks in the door to make sure no one was approaching. One time, I observed some neighbour children wearing dresses made out of *taleisim*, prayer shawls. They probably had no idea what this represented; their mothers had likely bought them as pieces of good quality material. The marking and fringes of the *tallis* were clearly visible.

From time to time we were given some tasks to do, like husking beans and corn, or some hand-sewing, which we loved to do. From scraps of fabric we made dolls for Barbara. We stuffed the bodies with hay and dressed them up; Helen was good at embroidering the faces. When Barbara asked where the dolls came from, Emilia told her that she sewed them at night. Barbara remembers the dolls to this day.

I tried to relieve the daily stress in my own way. Once, when a young chick wandered into our stable, I started feeding it with whatever was available, like husked corn or oats taken from the horse's trough. I dreamt that when the chick grew up, it would surely make a nest in the stable and lay eggs. It kept coming to the stable even with the door closed, just through a little crack. If the door was tightly shut, it would stay on the stoop, even in the rain. It turned out to be a rooster, but I loved it anyway. I still have its feather. I believed it was my good luck omen.

There was a time one early spring, March, when the earth started thawing and the result was that water seeped into our hiding box. We were lying on very wet straw, which became mouldy; there was no way to change the straw altogether, but we did take out handfuls of it at night, covered it with horse's manure, and supplemented it by stealing from the horse's bedding. It was no use complaining about it; there were bigger concerns and problems all around us. The fleas and lice were all over us, crawling freely, and we would pick them off each other. It was a losing battle, but we persisted anyway. We also picked each other's hair lice.

In the summer, food was more plentiful. Sometimes Victor cut off a whole bush of sweet peas and deposited it on the stable floor. For the next few days we picked the stalks full of fresh peas. Sometimes he'd bring some rutabagas and we would keep busy slicing off chunks of the vegetable. Late one summer, he brought a basket of apples that had fallen off the trees before ripening. We devoured this treat and I must have overdone it because I developed a terrific bellyache. I was in terrible pain, and we suspected appendicitis. We had no choice but to tell Emilia and ask for some medicine. All she could offer were a couple of headache powders. I continued having strong pains. Victor was concerned that I would die and that he would have no choice but to bury me close by on the property. At that time they were more concerned about having a grave on the property than about my possible recovery. But recover I did.

Another time, Helen developed a toothache from an infected tooth. Her face was swollen and she was in severe pain. She begged Victor to pull the tooth out and promised not to make any noise. So he brought some pliers and pulled the tooth out, but it was the wrong tooth. So she said, you might as well pull out the bad tooth now, which he did.

One day Victor came with some food, very disturbed and aggravated. He had been ploughing the field close to the boundary strip dividing the neighbours' properties. The neighbour accused him of making the boundary strip narrower, therefore taking a strip from their soil. He was accused again of hiding Jews. He was shaking and did not know what to do next. He was on the verge of letting us go but somehow held himself back for a day or two and did not even share this incident with his sister. Things quieted down after a while. Until the next scare.

I think that most of the hidden Jews survived in the villages. In the towns there were not many places to hide, though there were some Jews who survived in hiding against all odds. One of our friends who survived by hiding on a farm was a little boy, approximately nine years of age. His protectors were being paid from time to time. His parents arranged it so that another farmer held the money or valuables. Often the boy was dressed as a Polish farm girl and went to collect the next payment. He was blond and blue-eyed, so it was easier to hide him.

In the bigger cities some Jews survived on what were called "Aryan" papers. If they spoke good Polish and had a Slavic look, they took on an image of just another Polish person. They would obtain some falsified documents, such as a birth certificate and church papers showing a baptismal certificate, and they learned the prayers and attended church regularly to blend in. Some had Polish friends who helped them with the paperwork or in securing a job, and they tried to be part of the community. Some did survive that way; others were betrayed as a fraud, and that was the end of them.

In the little towns and villages, the situation was somewhat different. Some Jews had been farmers and had lived the same way as the Poles, so they could not just mingle in a crowd. Some of the farmers had business dealings with the small-town Jews and had even been friendly with them, if not friends. Other Jews were known in the villages from their constant travel with their wagons filled with household goods for sale. On a farm, there are outbuildings, like a barn, a stable, a tool shed; I think there are many more places to hide than in the city, and even though the food supply may not have been plentiful, it was not on ration cards and therefore not so controlled by the authorities.

When we heard that Jews were found hiding in the fields or the woods, we assumed they had been thrown out by someone who would not protect them any longer. Obviously Jews could not have survived for two years in the open; someone had been protecting them for a while, either until they reached a breaking point or until the Jews had nothing else to give or promise to give.

~

In mid-1944, the Soviet offensive was on the move. For a while it seemed that, according to the censored newspaper, the Soviet army was advancing somewhat. We knew it was true when leaflets were dropped from an aircraft to warn the population not to resist and to help the Soviet army when they got closer. Around this time, we were faced with a tragedy that hit close to home. In the middle of the day, as children were returning from school, a foreign aircraft dropped a couple of small bombs on the little town of Dąbrowa. One of Emilia's children, Antoni, was hit by shrapnel. He was quite wounded, and since there was no hospital in Dąbrowa, Victor and Emilia packed him up on the horse-drawn wagon and took him to the nearest hospital in Tarnów. He had injuries on his legs and back and was in danger for quite a while. Antibiotics and penicillin were unavailable, and only disinfectant was used, his wounds cleaned to prevent infection. This situation directly affected us — there was even less time for our needs, and we were completely neglected. We knew the child was their priority now, and rightly so; however, there we were without any food supplies. It took a few days before Victor showed up with some water and food to keep us from starving. It took the child a few weeks to recover and he still bears the scars.

Next, the German army soldiers started showing up in and around Dąbrowa. They came to our village and set up camps in the fields — their field kitchens — and brought a lot of heavy Arabian horses. They came into our stable and parked their horses, then made themselves at home in Emilia's one-room cottage, sometimes just to warm up. What about us, stuck there under the stable? Victor was at his wit's end about what to do. We were sitting or, rather, lying down like that proverbial mouse under the broom. This would surely be the end of us.

But resourceful Victor was not about to give up now, when he sensed that the war was turning against the Germans. He figured he was not going to waste two years of his efforts and daily horror for naught. So he put up a few planks of wood in the attic above the cottage in one corner, made a small lean-to and covered it up with the hay that was stored there. In the middle of the night he guided us through the courtyard into the attic and into the prepared corner. The corner adjoined the attic above the pigsty, so he hacked out a small opening in the floor between the beams to make a provision for our toilet needs. We could now sit up and even stand up in one place because the roof was slanted.

We could hear the German soldiers all around us. They were everywhere — at the neighbours, in our courtyard — but they didn't bother the local population; they just took what they found available in the way of food. When we spread apart a small crack of the thatched roof, we could almost touch the soldiers, they were that close. Their job was not, however, to flush out Jews; they just went about their own orders. Sometimes the family was given food from their field kitchen and Emilia brought us some of their leftovers. Now one of our biggest concerns was how to avoid making any noise that was beyond our control, like a cough or a sneeze.

In late November and December it was cold, and occasionally one of the soldiers took the liberty of sleeping in the cottage. Our pitcher of water froze overnight many times, so we took to sleeping with the pitcher between us, under our covers. Strangely, we never suffered from catching a cold, even though we were freezing many a night.

It was nearing Christmas when an order appeared for all able men and boys to report for digging ditches for the soldiers in preparation for an expected battle. They were ordered to go a few miles east and Victor was gone for about two weeks. Emilia was left to cope with everything on her own. After ten days of digging trenches, Victor returned, worn out, but well and somewhat optimistic. He greeted us by saying, "Are you still alive?" He saw with his own eyes that the war was turning. We said a special prayer after his return. There were more leaflets being dropped from planes now, informing the population that the glorious Soviet army was on its way to liberate us.

For a few days in January 1945 it suddenly got very quiet. When the German soldiers started packing up their equipment, we did not know what to make of it. Eventually, they took Emilia's only horse and a cow and left. Now Emilia and Victor had no means of transportation and wondered how they would manage. We could hear some distant guns firing; it sounded as though it was coming from heavy equipment like cannons. People were at a loss as to how to prepare for whatever was coming next. There was no information of any kind available. Even the censored press had stopped printing. Then, for about three days, it got even quieter than it had been before. Even the damn flies had died off, and we could hear only the cows moo or the roosters crow. People stuck close to their homes, waiting. Suddenly, we could hear the distant sounds of vehicles or trucks moving; there was a vibration in the earth, and then we could distinguish the smell of car exhausts. Someone came and spread the news that Russian soldiers had been spotted.

When Victor came and relayed the news to us, he said that we could start relaxing now. "It seems that the German soldiers have vanished swiftly, like the wind," he said. However, he decided to keep us hidden for a few days more, just in case. He was not going to take a risk and release us prematurely. Finally, one day Emilia brought the children up to the attic to reveal our presence there. Naturally, they were stunned. We started to hug and kiss them, but they resisted; after all, they did not know us any more, and they didn't know what to make of the whole thing. Luckily, they were too young to realize what danger they had been in for the last two and a half years because of us. Years later, one of them said that they did hear some strange noises and creaks coming from the attic at night but decided to keep quiet about it, thinking it must have been ghosts up there. I guess we were ghosts, though ghosts alive.

Next, Victor went to town to assess the situation. He came back to report that a few Jews had already "crawled out of the holes" as he put it, and the community had found for them a couple of rooms to live in. Since he had claimed to his neighbours throughout the war that he was not hiding Jews, he decided not to let them know otherwise just yet. He said that the best way for us to leave the farm would be to walk into town under cover of night. We could then return in a little while during the day, when it would seem like we were coming to visit old acquaintances. And so it was.

The Survivors

We marched the few miles to town on a bitterly cold January night, practically naked, and I believe that's when I got the first of the bladder infections that would plague me for many years to come. Not much had been available in terms of clothing for us. Most of the clothes from our last apartment were by then worn out or non-existent. Emilia had dug out some old raincoats. That night, I was wearing a pair of men's shoes, a nightgown and a raincoat. No underwear, no stockings. Helen wore similar things. We each had a piece of fabric that we used as a kerchief; that was all.

It took a long while for it to sink in that we were actually free. We searched out the small group of survivors — there were about ten of us — and we lived together in a tiny flat and exchanged our survival stories. Some of the townspeople brought us some food and a few articles of used clothes. We had no means of supporting ourselves and lived only on handouts. We shared everything.

I then recalled that some of our family's articles were buried under the floor in the studio. We decided to dig them up, and a couple of local police officers went to the studio with us because it was occupied. We removed a couple of floorboards and retrieved the buried objects. There were candlesticks, wine cups, silver cutlery and the head of the sewing machine; alas, everything had rusted after almost three years. Most of the clothes fell apart on being lifted out. Some clothes survived and could be worn after a good wash and exposure to the sun. There were also some cooking utensils, possibly things that had been used only for Pesach, because they were in good shape. We handed over most of the items to Emilia but kept some of the pots and pans for ourselves, so our little group of survivors was able to cook whatever was available.

We kept a communal style of living out of sheer necessity. A few more survivors started to appear, from further villages or forests, and everyone was taken in, regardless of the lack of space. We were so accustomed to hardship that there was no problem with sleeping arrangements; we slept wherever there was an empty spot on the floor.

I was in terrible pain from the bladder infection, and the only remedy someone came up with was for me to sit on a hot steamy pot. No one thought of searching for a doctor, and I wonder if one was available. The relief agencies were not yet set up; we had been gloriously free since the end of January 1945, but the war was still in progress until May 1945.

Victor came to visit us on Sundays after church and regaled everyone with his stories of how he outwitted the Germans. One of his favourite tales was about the time when the Arabian horses were led into the stable and the floor collapsed in one spot under the weight of one horse and revealed our box underneath. The two soldiers were very curious as to why the box was there, but since they did not speak Polish and Victor knew no German, he tried to explain to them with gestures, trying to convey that he had prepared it for his family if, "Boom boom boom," the bombs were threatening. He relished repeating the same incidents over and over and enjoyed it even more if he had a large audience and their attention.

Other facts came to the surface. I had forgotten one episode, but when Victor brought it up, it stirred my memory. Early in our hiding, I had approached Victor when he was delivering food to us. I kissed his hands and said, "Our only hope, sir, is in you." Just a spontaneous sentence. It was only then, during one of his visits, that he admitted it had stuck in his head and that was why he had tried so hard to save us.

It was there in Dąbrowa, among our group, that I first experienced feelings for one young survivor, and we were seen together all the time. We promised each other to keep in touch when our lives got straightened out. We did meet later that year in Krakow, but it was not the same anymore. Then, about two years later, we coincidentally met on a train in Germany and realized that what we had had was a fleeting romance, a celebration of survival, and that we did not mean anything to each other any longer.

Other things surfaced. I found out about my mother's fate from a man who knew my family and recognized me. He had been in the Tarnów ghetto in 1943 and told me what he knew. As I mentioned, my mother was also in the ghetto in Tarnów, illegally, because she had snuck in with my brother. One day the German police were apparently looking for a man who had not shown up for forced labour. They searched the apartment building where my mother was living. She didn't know what they were looking for, but just in case she hid in a wardrobe. They found her and shot her on the spot. They were not in the habit of asking questions. I wasn't able to find out the date, nor what happened to my little brother. That was the only information I got from the man. He had witnessed many shootings and could not recall any more details. He himself survived in hiding and was the only one from his entire family to survive.

Around the same time, I was approached by one of the newly arrived survivors who told me he was aware of who I was, and that he knew some members of my family. He pointed this out to me right after we had dug up the hidden stuff from under the floorboards. I was unaware that the little building in which the studio was located originally belonged to my maternal grandmother and then was transferred to her daughter Frania, my aunt. He told me this information and said that since I was the only direct survivor, the little building ought to pass on to me. He was familiar with the local authorities, so he offered to try to transfer the ownership to me if I would let him sell it. He would get half of the value. I signed some papers, he sold it, and as far as I was concerned it was like found money, though I was surely taken advantage of and cheated. At least we now had a little cash.

In the spring, some of the survivors figured out when Pesach would arrive and the group decided that we would keep the tradition and refrain from eating bread. The logistics of how this was accomplished escape me, but somehow flour was obtained, as well as the use of a bakery oven. All of us participated, rolling the dough with bottles, and my job was to criss-cross the matzos with a wheel from a watch.

After Pesach, we started to think about what to do next. Actually, Helen did all the thinking; I just followed her plan. One of the survivors, a man who was originally from Krakow, travelled there and wrote us that a Jewish committee was being formed to help the survivors. He also informed us that he had joined the committee and was therefore assigned a room and a kitchen, which he shared with another friend. If we wished to join him in Krakow, he would provide a little space for us as well. We used some of our money to travel to Krakow. He managed to prepare for us a single bed, which we shared. We spent our precious money carefully, but we had to have a comforter for our bed, so we bought a used one on the black market.

Our first task was to go to the committee, register and ask for any help that was available. The committee was located in a three-storey building and it was a meeting place for all of us survivors. I even remember the address, Długa 38. The place was a lifesaver for all the survivors in Krakow. Besides housing a common kitchen where some simple food could be obtained, or some used donated clothes, it contained offices where the staffers had the good sense to collect various stores of information from the survivors, as well as parodies of songs and poems made up in the camps. Everything was still fresh in our collective minds. Helen and I submitted some of our poems.

We also registered our names on the survivors' list. The committee tried — through the Red Cross or Jewish organizations like the Hebrew Immigrant Aid Society (HIAS) — to connect us with relatives in other countries, mostly America. The organizations did an excellent job, and many people were connected that way. Inquiries were already pouring in from overseas, mostly from the US. People were searching for the fate of their relatives. Through the efforts of the committee, my second cousin Martha found us. She was living in Northern Rhodesia, which later became Zambia. It did not take long for a couple of Helen's cousins who lived in New York to also locate us. Within months, they started sending us parcels, mostly used clothes, which had double value; they were not just for our personal use but also for resale on the black market. Used clothes were very much in demand, especially good American material and styles, as people were anxious to buy something different from what they had during the war, when new things were not being manufactured. Also, after six years, most people's clothes were simply worn out. Some people were retrieving clothes or valuables from Polish families, things that had been left with them for safekeeping. Some gave these back willingly while others made excuses, like claiming their belongings had been stolen. Articles like nylon stockings had high value, as did lipstick. These things could only be bought on the black market at a high price. Helen made daily trips to the market, with me tagging along, carrying the merchandise.

The Jewish committee also tried to collect names of the persecutors in the death camps and any other scraps of information on them, possibly for the purpose of bringing them to justice at a later time. They also wanted the names of Jewish prisoners who had had some limited privileges in the camps to help their brethren, in some small way, but did not, and chose to be crueller than they needed to be. These people were called kapos, a kind of overseer. Not all were cruel, but those who were were well known to some survivors, and later, when the State of Israel was established, these kapos did not dare to immigrate there or even visit Israel, because they feared for their lives. I know of two of these survivors who live in Toronto. Cruelty has no borders. They will be looked upon with contempt and scorn for the rest of their lives.

When the war ended, a stream of death camp survivors started arriving in Krakow, searching and searching, trying to figure out what to do next. I met a couple of girls who had attended my school before the war. Their heads were shaved clean, their bodies skin and protruding bones, and I thought that we had not been so bad off. A young man, David, who lived with us in the flat, found two of his cousins, sisters, and he invited them to join our little place. It was getting really cramped; we had just our bed and one chair, and our only possession was a knife, which we kept together with our loaf of bread in the corner of the bed. We felt good knowing that we could have a slice of bread anytime. Since we had no cooking facilities we lived mostly on bread, whatever vegetable or fruit could be purchased, and ice cream cones.

I soon met a young man who had come to visit someone in our group, and he invited me out for a walk and an ice cream. He was quite a bit older but very attentive to me, and in retrospect I think he enjoyed my youth — I was only fifteen — innocence and naïveté. We had a bit of a romance. He called on me many times that summer, and we walked the streets of the city we both loved or sat in parks or on the bank of the Vistula River. He was a hairdresser by trade and planned in time to establish himself and make a good living. I think he was on the verge of proposing, but then during one of our conversations he revealed that he had been married before the war and had two young children; he thought that his wife had survived in Czechoslovakia, but he said that if they ever met, he planned to divorce her. That information turned me off. Later, I wondered why Helen never warned me about anything to do with men. Even though I had no secrets from her, she knew all there was to know. Perhaps she had problems of her own to solve.

Helen was a very social person and made friends very easily; she liked people and she had a certain charm and charisma. I was definitely not in her league at all. Sometimes I resented the fact that these new-found friends took her away from me. I wanted to have exclusive rights on her time. I was accepted mostly as a package deal — wherever she went, I went.

I tagged along to the market daily, until an acquaintance of ours suggested that I ought to be instead sent to school. My education was badly lacking. A new facility was being set up in one of the public schools to accommodate the young survivors whose education had been so abruptly interrupted with the outbreak of the war, when Jewish children were barred from school. There was one class for all of us, of different ages, and some of us did not even have basic reading or math skills. I was very eager to learn anything. The teacher was also a survivor, and she understood our feelings and our frustrations. I spent about a year learning a smattering of different subjects and even passed an exam at the end.

After school I had another project going. Helen bought some remnants of fabric at the market, and I fashioned them by hand into rag dolls. I already had some experience from the times in the stable when we had sewn dolls for Barbara. First, a body had to be stitched together, legs, arms, then head, and then it was stuffed with sawdust or wood shavings. We sewed them dresses, and Helen was still good at embroidering the faces. The last step was selling them at the market, and we did quite well. So well, in fact, that in time we were able to rent our own room in someone's apartment. At one point we tried to find real jobs and, with someone's help, we were hired to work in a glass factory where various tubes were manufactured, but we got little training, and after a couple of weeks we were fired. From time to time a few dollars came in a letter from America, and that was a real bonus.

As I mentioned, making friends came easily and naturally to Helen, and she forged meaningful relationships with men as well as women. One of the men she befriended often came to visit us at our one-room apartment. He was well-dressed even then, and quite elegant. I don't know what he did, maybe some smuggling or other illegal transactions, but he was good-looking and Helen fell in love with him. He was pleasant to me as well. They were seeing each other for a while before he confessed that he was living with a girlfriend but wanted to dump her and be with Helen. They decided that the best way to accomplish this would be if we left Krakow and travelled to the American zone in West Germany, where Displaced Persons (DP) camps were being set up and food was supplied. Crossing the border illegally was not too difficult because a Jewish organization called Bricha had been formed to help Jews reach British Mandate Palestine, and if we joined one of its associated Zionist groups, like Mizrachi, Hashomer Hatzair or Dror, they would look after us until we eventually landed in Palestine.

In the late summer of 1946, Helen and I went to visit Victor and Emilia to say our goodbyes for the last time, and then we travelled to a small town on the border of Czechoslovakia, which was the gathering place for crossing the border. Helen's boyfriend was to follow next day; it was his suggestion that we not leave Krakow together. Helen and I arrived in the town and joined the first organization that we stumbled upon; I think it was Dror. There was a few days' waiting time until the next border crossing would be arranged. Helen and I walked all around town looking for her boyfriend, and we were quite puzzled that we could not locate him. He did not arrive the next day or the day after, or the day after that, and we thought that the worst had happened to him. We were in a quandary and distraught over what to do next. When the day arrived that the border crossing was to take place, we decided to cross with our Dror group, hoping it was some kind of misunderstanding and that we would connect with him on the other side. It took us some time to reconcile to the idea that we had just been dumped, abandoned by him. We found ourselves at a point of no return. There was nothing for us to go back to, since we had given up our room and taken our few possessions with us. Our most treasured possession was our notebook with addresses of relatives in the US.

Helen still deluded herself that the whole thing was some crossed signals, and she looked forward to joining up on the other side. Crossing the border was a process done under cover of night; we had to be smuggled through. We had no passports or any identity papers, and neither did any of the other refugees. We entered through Czechoslovakia and were next sent to Vienna, which was the transit point. From there, we were sent to another transit camp in Austria, about one hundred and fifty kilometres from the city of Linz.

This camp, in the town of Puch bei Hallein, was located at the foot of a mountain and was surrounded by mountains. The area was breathtaking — the snow-covered mountains and brisk fresh air — though very few of us had much appreciation for the scenery, as other concerns were on our minds. The DP camp was a collection of barracks, and each one of us was assigned to a room and issued an army cot, a pillow and a blanket. That was all. There were quite a variety of people in each room, some married couples, but most were single men, women and young adults, about ten to a room. A pot-bellied stove was in every room and we stoked it with whatever fuel was available. When the fire went out at night, it was freezing, and we shivered under our only blanket. Someone would often get up in the middle of the night to re-stoke the little stove. The toilets were in the main building, too far to venture out on cold nights, and most of us just relieved ourselves right outside the barracks. But since we were being fed daily — meals were provided in the communal dining hall — there were no complaints about the lack of sanitary conditions. After all, this was just a transit camp, and we had been through much worse still fresh in our collective memories.

One of the people assigned to our room was Leizer (Lester). He had come from the Soviet Union, where he had spent the war, and his destination was uncertain, as was ours. While passing through Poland he had also searched the survivor lists and discovered that two of his nephews survived the concentration camps and were in Germany. His plan was to locate them and meet them.

We spent a few weeks in this transit camp, after which truckloads of us were shipped to Traunstein in southeastern Bavaria, Germany, about one hundred kilometres from Munich. Before we left, someone advised me to invest the money I had saved from the sale of my grandmother's little studio house. Some of the money had been used for our immediate, urgent needs, like our travel to Krakow, and with the balance Helen and I bought some gold coins. They were called English Sovereigns, and these were our security blanket. Helen had a compartment built into the heel of her shoe and hid the coins there. When I later left for Canada, I left the coins with her, still in her shoe. Helen eventually immigrated to the US with her husband, Lester, and their little boy, Raymond. The shoe was still with her. One day, Lester decided to throw out a bunch of old shoes, and it was then that she revealed to him that it was a valuable shoe and the coins were removed. She later recounted the story to me in letters. We corresponded all the time, until her untimely death in 1956. I wish I knew what happened to those gold coins. Perhaps Lester still had them in his possession when he died in 1999. I must ask his sons if they came across them when they cleared out his apartment. I would love to have one of these coins; it would be quite a souvenir.

At the beginning of 1947, we arrived in the town of Traunstein, where there was an abandoned military compound. The barracks were elegant and had likely been for officers only. The compound consisted of seven three-storey buildings, or blocks, as they came to be known, and was being set up as a refugee receiving camp. Everyone was to register and was assigned a room. Families were kept together, though if they had a large room, two or more families had to share it. To create some semblance of privacy, people separated their space by hanging blankets. There were toilets on each floor and there was a common shower room, army style. Leizer, Helen and I were assigned to a small room. In time, Leizer tracked down his two nephews and met with them.

There were endless lines for everything in the camp — the daily food rations from the communal kitchen, access to toilets and showers, and other supplies that were distributed from time to time. We spent many hours just waiting. Most of us had an empty juice can container for which we fashioned a wire handle, and this was how we collected our rations. We could then take our food and eat in our room. The rooms were sparsely furnished — army cots, a couple of lockers, the odd chair or table. We were supplied with bedding and soap and towels, which was a luxury for us. Leizer became one of the committee members and always managed to get something extra. He even got a hot plate, which was envied by others.

We had no special destination or outlook for the future. The ways to Palestine were blocked, and so most of us just stayed in the camp. I think it was the United Nations Relief and Rehabilitation Administration (UNRRA) and other organizations that provided for our needs. Some people held jobs in the camp and were reimbursed, thus having extra income to supplement what the camp was providing; after all, only our basic needs were provided for. Helen became a teacher in the camp's school, on the premises, and Leizer was also working, so we usually had some money to go into town and buy whatever was available. An Organization for Rehabilitation through Training (ORT) school opened up to teach young girls some skills, and I took up sewing and also took English lessons.

It was through the search lists that Helen found out that her brother Josef had survived the war in the Soviet Union and was now in western Germany, in another Displaced Persons camp in the British zone, in Bergen-Belsen. It was a shock to find him, and he eventually came to meet us. We filled in all the missing years, and Helen asked him to come and live with us and share our room. During the few days that he stayed, we cried for all our lost family members. We told him all that we knew and what had happened to his wife, Frania, and their two children, Janus and Krysia. Josef had escaped to the Soviet Union in late 1939, and we described what life was like after he left, up until Frania and the children were taken to be murdered in June 1942.

When Helen urged him to stay with us for good, he confessed that he had met a survivor of the Bergen-Belsen concentration camp, a woman for whom he cared very much, and was planning to marry her. Dora was her name, and she was as short as he was tall. He went back to Bergen-Belsen, and after a while they both came back to Traunstein in order for us to meet Dora. They then married and lived in Bergen-Belsen until it was decided what our next destination would be.

We could not live in the DP camps forever, but after all the hardships people lived through, be it in the Soviet Union, death camps, hiding or living in the forests, we were relatively comfortable in the Traunstein camp. We were also scared and reluctant to try to look for other avenues in order to leave. Life seemed good. The camp even supplied some entertainment — musicians came about once a week and even American entertainers showed up. It was a self-contained little community. Many young people met and married there and had babies; some privileged couples got a room to themselves. Some people started immigrating to England and France, where they had found relatives, but not many could immigrate to America.

Helen, ever effervescent, had quite a few marriage proposals along the way, and I even kept a record of the names of these rejected suitors. The last two very serious contenders were in the Traunstein DP camp. One was Leizer, and the other was also an upstanding young man; they were both vying for Helen's hand in marriage. None of us was getting involved in her decision, not even her brother Josef; she had to make up her own mind and she chose Leizer, for reasons known only to herself. I liked both of them and would have accepted either one; however, I was not asked for advice, nor did I offer any. Whatever Helen did was all right with me. She was my mentor and I trusted her judgment on everything. We had a little ceremony, wine and sponge cakes were arranged, and that was it.

A New World of Wonders

It was now the beginning of 1948, and I felt kind of lost. Somehow Uncle Josef found out that registrations were being held in Munich for orphaned children and youth, and he pushed me to go and register for eventual immigration to America, so I did. He always joked with me because I hated to get up at dawn to catch the train to Munich, and when I complained, he said, "All right, tomorrow you will have to get up early, and then again when you travel to America, and then you won't have to get up early anymore." After I registered to immigrate and was accepted, I was asked where I wanted to go and I said America, but the interviewers told me that the quota was full. However, I could register for Canada, so I agreed.

I was then sent to a temporary holding camp, a so-called children's camp, which was really two old hotels converted for our use. I lived there for about six months before my group was shipped to Canada. The camp was in the little town of Prien. We went to school there, on the premises, and the classes were geared to our level. We made lasting friendships, and in 1998 we had our fiftieth reunion there. By then we were scattered throughout the US and Canada.

Here's the story of our coming to Canada: at that time, the Canadian government was very much against admitting Jews in general, but after a lot of pressure from the Canadian Jewish community, particularly the Canadian Jewish Congress, a government act was passed and they relented to admit about 1,000 Jewish orphans, survivors from war-torn Europe, on condition that the Jewish community would not allow them to become burdens on the country, that they be relatively healthy, especially free of tuberculosis and eye disease, and that they be under eighteen years of age. There was a scramble of how to get us to Canada in time — the urgency was that so many of us were approaching our eighteenth birthday, and ships were not easily available. Doctors were assigned to examine us and X-rays had to be taken, as well as urine samples; the doctors were not in a particular rush, but we were. Some administrators connected with our eventual departure had to be bribed. Nothing was on the straight and narrow — birthdates were changed and documents falsified. Everything was still in turmoil.

There were a few social workers trying to prepare us for what was forthcoming, but in retrospect I think we took little notice. We were street smart, and we learned how to lie smoothly to suit our purposes. But the friendships we made were the genuine article. To overcome the difficulties the examining doctors presented some of us with, we resorted to our cunning ways. One of our group, a young girl, was being held back because the doctor reported finding a spot on her lungs, which made her ineligible to travel. So her friend went to another examining doctor in her friend's place, had her X-rays taken, and was passed. Now both were admitted. We were supposed to be "fully orphaned," but some of us were only partly orphaned — the surviving parent wanted their child to have a better chance to emigrate, since the future was as yet uncertain for the grownups. We shared our confidences with each other, without any fear of being betrayed.

The Jewish families who signed up for taking in a young boy or girl had an image in their minds of getting a young child whom they could care for and send to school. What they got instead was a group of sad-faced adolescents with whom they could not even converse, and who had their own ideas and demands. We were all a troublesome bunch.

In my transport group were approximately one hundred young people, and while en route to Canada we were divided into smaller groups. If anyone had a relative in Canada and knew their address, they were to be located in that city. If we had no one, they just divided us all across Canada, wherever there were Jewish families who agreed to take in a youngster. I was to travel to Sydney, Nova Scotia, for no particular reason. I had no quarrel with it, especially since my best friend, Betty, was also assigned to travel to Sydney. I was so happy that we had not been split up.

While on the ship, we were served food three times a day that was foreign to us — cornflakes, oatmeal, juices and generous portions of meat that we had no experience with in our memories. In the centre of the table there was a bowl of apples, enough for each person at the table. We eyed those apples, making sure that no one took more than one. This was a real delicacy.

In June 1948, we arrived in Halifax, where social workers were to pick us up. Since a number of us were assigned to Sydney, we spent a few days as temporary guests in private homes awaiting the arrival of social workers who were to escort us there. Betty and I ventured out around the neighbourhood, and the grocery stores amazed us. We could not figure out why oranges and cabbages were displayed side by side. Also, the sight of so much food available for purchase was remarkable. We each had five dollars, given to us on leaving the ship, and we certainly were not ready to spend it at that time. (I also had twenty dollars sewn into the shoulder pad of my dress, which was to be used for emergencies only.) The chocolate bars were pretty enticing, but we resisted.

During the next days we travelled by train with our social workers to Sydney and were delivered to our respective assigned families. The family whose home I was to share, Mr. and Mrs. E. Newman, had four teenage children, and they doubled up the two boys so that I could have a room to myself. The whole thing was a puzzle to me.

I was under the impression that I was being adopted into this family, but I could not comprehend why they would want another teenager when they already had two girls and two boys. The social workers failed to explain to us the meaning of a foster home, and neither did the family whose home I was sharing. I felt lost in this new world, full of wonders. I was told when to come down for meals, but I didn't have much interaction with the other children in the family or with their parents. I don't remember being asked many questions; it is possible that they were waiting for me to open up, but this was not my nature, and so we just existed side by side. I was asked to help with some household chores, which I did obediently. A bright point of my day was getting together with the others from my group, exchanging our feelings and other information. None of us knew what to do or what to expect next.

Our local social worker, Mrs. Nina Cohen, was a wonderful person. She herself was coping with young Joseph, one of our group, and she encountered some extra problems that she had not bargained for. Joseph had an older brother still in Germany, who had not been able to come with us because he was a few years older. Joseph begged Mr. and Mrs. Cohen to help bring his brother to Canada. They must have pulled some strings because after a while Sigmund showed up in Sydney, and the Cohens took him in. Now they had two young adults who needed a lot of attention and adjustment. Mrs. Cohen sensed our loneliness and managed to invite the whole bunch of us to their home for dinners, and even to their summer cottage. She was one in a million and is fondly remembered by all of us to this day.

The local Jewish shopkeepers offered to outfit us with one new set of clothes, and I was allowed to pick out one dress and a winter coat. That summer, I got my first job in a ladies' wear store. It was late summer and sales were in progress to move the summer merchandise. My job was to watch for shoplifters. Whether I did a good job of it or for my employers' own reasons, they offered me a job in one of the departments selling underwear, girdles, bras and stockings. I was thrilled with my first pay packet. When I came home I was in a quandary as to whether to offer part of my pay to my hosts, and after consulting with Betty, I did. The Newmans suggested I save the money, telling me that I was not a boarder, another strange expression I was not familiar with. What was I? Total confusion. They helped me to open a bank account.

My employers, Mr. and Mrs. Jacobson, were quite kind to me. One day Mr. Jacobson took me aside and told me he'd pay me a few extra dollars on the side every week, which he did not want the other employees to know about. I was now sending a dollar or two in a letter to Helen in Germany. Mr. and Mrs. Jacobson even sent me to Halifax for a short course about selling underwear and it was all expenses paid, even the hotel. I felt like I belonged.

After living with the Newman family for a few months, working and learning about Canada, the first book I tackled was *Gone with the Wind*. I also went to the movies with my friends. Life seemed good. Across the street from where I lived with the Newmans was a variety store and the owner, Mr. Jack Moraff, ran it by himself. His older brother had immigrated to Sydney before the war, and when Jack surfaced after surviving the war in the Soviet Union, his brother had sent the necessary papers. Jack was hard-working and a smart businessman; he added various items to his store that were selling well, like children's toys and ice cream. When a child came in asking what ice cream flavours were available, Jack used to say, "I have all flavours." Actually, he had the three basic ones — vanilla, strawberry and chocolate. When the child wanted maple walnut, he just mixed up the chocolate and vanilla and said it was maple walnut. He didn't have much of a social life yet, so he kept the store open long after the other stores closed for the night. Financially, he was doing quite well.

I was introduced to him when he dropped into the Newmans. He asked me out a few times, and I enjoyed it. The Newmans tried talking me into considering marrying him, even though he was quite a bit older. Mr. Moraff told me quite a bit about himself — how he escaped to the Soviet Union when the war broke out, leaving behind a wife and a young child. He was very bitter about losing his child and about so many children being killed in general, and he decided he would not have any more children in his life. He proposed to me and I said I would think about it, but in fact I had made up my mind that I would not marry anyone who told me up front that he did not want children. A few months later I left for Toronto, and he wished me well. For many years later we exchanged New Year's cards, until one day I got a letter from one of his nieces informing me that he had died. Another chapter of my life had closed.

One Sunday, my social worker, Mrs. Cohen, called me and said she wanted to take me out for lunch, just by myself. I was puzzled, because we were used to doing things in groups. She took me out for lunch and then just drove around for a while before bringing me back. Before I had a chance to thank her and get out of the car, she informed me that I was no longer welcome to stay with the Newmans. Apparently, Mrs. Newman had complained that it was too much for her to have another person in the house. I was not to worry, another home would be located for me. I was quite shaken and I felt abandoned once again. When I returned "home" not a word was mentioned by the Newmans, or for that matter by me. It was as if my conversation with Mrs. Cohen had never happened.

A few days later I was told to pack my things, and Mrs. Cohen took me to another home. I was told by the Newmans not to be a stranger, and even now when I hear these words it brings back the pain and the hurt of being told I was no longer welcome.

Luckily for me, the next home was warm and truly welcoming. The couple themselves knew firsthand the experience of not being wanted. The McPhails were fine people; Mr. McPhail, a Polish gentile, was an auto mechanic, his wife, Becky, was Jewish, and upon their marriage neither of their families wanted to have anything to do with them. Becky's parents had disowned her. The McPhails confided in me that they married for love and knew it would be a tough road, but they had not realized just how tough. They were music lovers and that's what had brought them together; they told me they were stared at even at a concert. They had two school-aged children and we all got along quite well.

I was to pay them part of my room and board, and the Canadian Jewish Congress picked up the balance. That arrangement suited us all very well. For many years later I corresponded with them, and they even visited me once in Toronto. They restored my faith in the goodness of people. My friend Betty had a similar experience; her second home was a good place to be. I don't recall the reason why Betty decided to travel to Toronto, but she did, and her second family, the Blonders, even funded her ticket, which was quite an expense. When she left, I felt very lonely. I was always a one-friend person, and I decided to follow her to Toronto, especially after she wrote me how much happier she was there, and that so many of our friends from the children's home were there. Betty described to me in glowing terms how they were all getting together and comparing notes about jobs and living accommodations.

By 1949, more of my friends in Sydney had started to leave. They claimed there was no future there. Some left for Montreal, others for Toronto. That's when I found out how far and expensive it would be to travel to Toronto. The only option was train travel, and it would take two days and two nights, and a berth had to be bought together with the ticket. When I had enough saved up, I approached Mrs. Cohen and asked how to go about travelling to Toronto. She contacted the Jewish Child and Family Service in Toronto, and they promised to find me a room when I arrived.

In Toronto I was on my own and, as arranged, a room was found for me with a Jewish family, the Richmans, on Palmerston Avenue. Living with the Richmans was a good experience for me. They treated me better than just a paying boarder. As in Sydney, the Canadian Jewish Congress subsidized part of my room and board because I did not earn enough at that time to cover my expenses.

An appointment was soon set up for me with a company engaged in manufacturing girdles and brassieres. However, they claimed I did not have enough experience in the field, which wasn't true. I sensed that antisemitism was the reason they wouldn't hire me. I eventually found a job on College Street in a dry goods store and worked there for quite a while. At night I attended night school, taking up shorthand and English. I wanted an office job, so I also took a typing course.

Meanwhile, I had a good time. I was reunited with my friend Betty and my friends from the children's home. Our entertainment was meeting on College Street and walking around, sometimes going to the movies. Everyone would tell stories of their progress and how they were adjusting to life in Canada. They seemed as happy to see me as I was to see them. They were like part of my family; we only had each other.

I started dating one of the boys, Rubin Applebaum, who paid a lot of attention to me, and we became what they call "an item." Rubin had been in our group of war orphans, although he was not at the children's home in Prien, Germany. We first met when we were being shipped by train to the German port of Bremen, and then we saw each other on the boat to Canada. He was living with his aunt and uncle to save on rent and was working in a clothes factory on Spadina. He had learned how to use a sewing machine and had become an operator. He was hard-working and did not mind working overtime and on holidays.

~

Idel Rubin Apfelbaum was born in a small shtetl near Sosnowiec, Poland. He was the youngest of four children and had two sisters, Miriam and Helen, and one brother, Moniek. Rubin's father, Nathan, was a ladies' wear tailor. His mother, Malka, was a homemaker. In those years, there were no ready-to-wear clothes available, or very few; however, fabrics could easily be purchased, with many stores dealing exclusively in textiles. Fashion magazines featuring pictures of the latest styles were quite popular. When a woman was ready for a new dress, suit or coat, she would peruse a magazine, pick out a style and then consult a tailor to find out how much fabric was required. She'd then purchase the fabric, bring it to the tailor and they'd agree on the price for the finished product. A couple of fittings were required before the dress, suit or coat was done.

The Apfelbaums' workshop was in one of the family's rooms, which usually served as sleeping quarters at night. Even with a family of six, there was not much space, mostly a room or two and a kitchen, and a common toilet was shared with a neighbour. Eking out a living was tough; there were not many customers in the small town, so the family decided to move to the large city of Warsaw, with the hope that work would be easier to obtain.

Rubin was very young at the time, about two years old, and he had no memories of the town he was born in. He grew up in Warsaw and he had very pleasant memories of his childhood. His father, as before, had his workshop at home, which was more economical. The older children were growing up, and the eldest girl, Miriam, married shortly before the war and had a baby.

When the war broke out in September 1939, the German Luftwaffe bombed Warsaw extensively. Rubin told me that one day, as they were sitting at dinner, a bomb hit the apartment building where they lived and their flat suffered heavy damage. In three weeks the German army overran Poland and took over many aspects of everyday life. Food rationing was one of the first edicts, and even on ration cards, it was necessary to stand in lines, sometimes for hours. This task was left to the children. They had a lot of time, as they were already forbidden to attend school, and even getting lessons privately was illegal.

One day, as his brother Moniek was waiting in line, a couple of German police came up and opened fire on the lineup of people, shooting indiscriminately. Moniek was shot and killed on the spot. When Rubin's father saw what was happening, he realized that the

Germans could kill with impunity. He then decided to try to save his younger son. In order to raise some money, he sold the sewing machine, which put him virtually out of business.

The mail was still operating as usual, and he got in touch with some of his family in the shtetl, asking if they'd make room for Rubin. Things were not as bad over there. With the money from selling the sewing machine, they packed Rubin up for the journey. Although the family received him warmly, there were circumstances beyond their control. Since he could not be registered legally, he did not have a ration card and had to be shielded from any inquiries. Whatever food there was now had to be shared with another person. This went on for a while, but in the end they all agreed that it was impossible to go on that way any longer. At that time, the Germans were looking for young people to willingly come forward and register to be sent to work camps in Germany. Rubin joined up.

At first, it was indeed work camps — slave labour, but not starvation rations yet. There were beatings and occasional shootings but not on a large scale. In 1942, when Hitler and his henchmen came up with the plan to systematically murder the Jewish population and death camps were established, Rubin went through several camps, one of them Auschwitz, where he was tattooed with the number B 10609. Being tattooed meant that the person was chosen for work, not immediate death.

The conditions were unbearable but, as he told me, he always managed to have a buddy, meaning they looked out for each other, protecting each other from other prisoners who were stealing whatever food portions they were saving and from other indignities that were taking place.

Although Rubin survived the war, shortly before the end of the war he became very ill and on liberation he was in the hospital. The liberating forces transferred the deathly ill prisoners to local hospitals; Rubin was treated for pleurisy and other starvation-induced illnesses. He was in the hospital for quite a long time, lying in bed and not being properly cared for. He subsequently suffered from bed-sores, which left permanent scars and indentations on many parts of his body — back, heels and other sensitive areas.

It was sometime after the war ended that Rubin's aunt in Canada, his mother's sister, found out that he was alive. His aunt's husband, Leib Noble, was a *melamed*, a Hebrew teacher, and one of his former students, J.B. Salsberg, was involved in provincial politics and was a member of the Ontario Legislature. Rubin's uncle approached Salsberg, and he was influential in helping to arrange Rubin's coming to Canada. It so happened that when a transport of orphans was scheduled to journey to Canada, he was included in the group. Since he had family in Toronto who guaranteed that he would not become a burden on Canadian institutions, he was assigned to travel there. His aunt and uncle were an Orthodox couple, parents of eight children — Gertie, Miriam, Ruth, Moishe, Florence, twins Blanche and Issie, and the youngest, Rosie — some of whom were still living at home, yet they readily made room for their nephew. They were very kind and were active in benevolent societies, but they were financially strapped.

Into this warm atmosphere, Rubin was embraced. He was helped to find a job and he worked on sportswear, doing piecework. As soon as he could afford it, he rented a room in a neighbour's house but continued to come for meals to his auntie. He became great friends with all his cousins.

~

Rubin and I were both working and trying to save every penny. There were so many temptations — clothes, movies — but we kept all spending to a minimum. Our utmost desire was to save as much as possible to enable us to become independent.

In 1950, a few months after we started dating, Rubin brought me home to meet his family — his auntie and uncle and the cousins. We all liked each other from the start, and I was received warmly. I can honestly say that I fell in love with his family. I was invited for Sunday lunches and for the seder at Pesach and was treated like one of the family.

Eventually, Rubin proposed marriage and convinced me that if we both kept working, we could afford to rent a flat of one room and a kitchen and start working ourselves up from there. I revealed that I hesitated to marry him because I did not love him — though I did like him — but he persuaded me that he loved me enough for the two of us and that I would learn to love him. I still had my doubts, but I did care for his family and looked forward to starting life as a couple. His auntie promised she'd arrange a shower for me; she had a lot of social contacts and I'd get a lot of useful items, which sounded very enticing.

It was shortly before we got engaged that he brought up the scars and indentations that covered most of his back, neck and heels. He felt it was only fair that I become acquainted with the way they looked and decide if they bothered me to the degree that I would wish to back out of the proposed engagement. He undressed and I examined them all. It was not a pretty sight. However, I said it would not stop me from going ahead with our plans. In all fairness, he did the right thing. He warned me that some activities like swimming or sunbathing would not be feasible for him, in order to avoid people staring. So, this matter was settled, and for years afterward I accepted it as just a part of him.

It was not until many years later that the scars became repulsive, turning me off, and sadly, I realized that the scars had not changed — it was my attitude, symptoms of something gone wrong. This became magnified, out of proportion. But that is another story, which will follow eventually.

Since Rubin could not afford a ring, he presented me with a watch as an engagement present. In June 1950, Rubin's uncle arranged for Rabbi David Ochs to marry us at the shul on D'Arcy Street, and the cousins got together to prepare a sweet table for the reception. The invitations were by word of mouth. There were not enough funds to splurge on wedding apparel; our budget would not allow for it. However, that problem was solved when a cousin, Celia Ostro, offered to lend me the gown and headpiece she had worn at her wedding the previous year. All our friends attended, and a mutual friend took some casual photos.

Rubin arranged a week's honeymoon in the nearby countryside. We had no way of getting there, and that was solved when one of the auntie's sons-in-law offered to drive us to our destination. When we arrived at the lodge, our first pleasant duty was to open the wedding envelopes and count the loot.

On our return, Rubin's auntie was instrumental in helping us find a flat, and we started working hard because we had spent some of our savings on a bedroom set and kitchen table and chairs. The spoils from the shower came in very handy and we bought bedding, towels, dishes and small appliances. We rented a stove and a fridge. Eventually, we bought a second-hand stove and fridge.

After our return from the countryside, a gentleman came to our flat and presented us with a bill for which we were ill-prepared. Rubin's uncle had arranged the shul and rabbi for us, and he had footed the bill. We weren't even aware that there was a fee to be paid for these services. We were quite green and did not know the local customs. The cousins, on the other hand, bought the items for the sweet table and decorated it themselves. At the wedding, some corsages and boutonnieres had been distributed to the wedding party, and some flowers placed on the sweet table. Most likely, the cousins had ordered these, but it was for these items that the florist presented us with a hefty bill. We were shocked and also embarrassed, since we didn't have enough funds to cover the bill. However, an arrangement was worked out and we paid it in installments over time.

It was summertime, and I was very fond of the warm weather, so I quit the salesgirl job and decided to take a few weeks off just to enjoy setting up a household and learning to cook. Eventually, I planned to find an office job. Rubin was very angry with my decision to quit my job and be a newlywed housewife for a while. He didn't approve of it. He worked on me and said that the sooner we started getting ahead the sooner we would be on "Easy Street." Eventually he persuaded me, although he did not convince me, and I started working in an office that summer. In retrospect, we were never on Easy Street, not according to his way of thinking. I was being brainwashed from the start without realizing it.

Awakening

Life went on. We had fun getting together with friends and going to a movie once in a while, though we were still trying to save wherever possible. We found a dressmaker who was good at turning over men's frayed collars, which saved us from having to buy new shirts. I still had my wardrobe from the time in Sydney when I worked in the ladies' wear store and as an employee was getting discounts on merchandise. Besides replacing a worn-out pair of shoes, little was spent on our personal apparel. Our goal was to save up enough for a down payment on a house, keep a couple of rooms for ourselves, and rent out the rest. That's what our friends were doing as well. The dream was to save up enough for that first house, and everything else was secondary in importance.

Our landlady had a wringer washer in the basement but had made us understand that we were not welcome to use it. And so, on the weekends, we gathered up our laundry in a pillowcase and, each of us holding one end, marched to the laundromat. Since I had an iron from the wedding shower, I ironed the clothes at home. We also cleaned on the weekends and dragged the groceries by hand from the market, only sometimes going by streetcar. But we didn't feel deprived, as all our friends were doing the same thing.

We were busy and happy establishing our new home, even though it consisted only of a room and a kitchen, with bathroom privileges. There was only one bathroom in the house on Borden Street, which was shared with the couple and their teenage son. We had been told from the start that showers and baths were allowed for us on Sundays only. It was also made clear that our shoes were to be taken off by the door, and should we have visitors they were to do likewise. We agreed to all the terms, the fact being that it was very difficult to rent a flat in those years. The demand was much bigger than the supply.

Sometimes we were surprised by our landlady's instructions. We were still new to Canadian ways. On the weekends in the summer, I liked to spread a blanket on the lawn in the backyard and sunbathe. However, I was told not to do this because that spot of grass would be flattened and the landlady did not like the idea. After living through the Holocaust and so many years of suffering and deprivation, it was just beyond our comprehension that some people would be upset by a spot of flattened grass.

After about a year, we were given notice to vacate because their son was getting married and the space was needed for him. We searched for another reasonable place and found one on Howland Avenue near Bloor Street, also a room and a kitchen, but there were disturbances there. The couple's two children had their bedrooms on the same floor as ours, and sometimes we could tell that someone had been in our rooms, most likely the children. We left the doors closed when leaving for work, but we weren't allowed to put locks on the doors. So we had aggravations of another kind, and we were more determined than ever to save every penny and deny ourselves whatever was not absolutely necessary to try to save for the down payment on a house.

We looked through the newspaper in the "Houses for Sale" columns but even a fixer-upper was still not within our reach. There was nothing to do except have a lot of patience and hope. It took us a couple of years of intense saving and resisting the many appealing items that we saw in store displays. I remember how I hated being wakened by the crude alarm clock each morning. I spotted a clock radio in an appliance store and eyed it every day on my way to work. Finally, the temptation of waking to music was too great, and we relented.

With the clock radio, we now had some entertainment and listened to various stories, news and music. There were even soap operas to get involved in, which were just like television without the video. On our free evenings we'd go to bed early and listen to the radio. We even entertained in our kitchen from time to time.

Finally the day arrived that we had just about enough for a down payment on a house. We found a house on Auburn Avenue, near St. Clair and Dufferin. We then realized we'd be short about a thousand dollars, since we had neglected to make provisions for legal costs and moving expenses. We had only the bedroom and kitchen sets, plus some boxes, but still, they had to be moved and paid for. An acquaintance offered us a loan at quite high interest, to be repaid within a year. It really cleaned us out, and we immediately advertised to rent out the upstairs three rooms. After we converted one of the rooms into a makeshift kitchen, the place was ready to be rented. Downstairs was a large kitchen, a dining room and a small living room. The kitchen we kept for ourselves, and the dining room served as a bedroom. The only toilet and bath were upstairs, to be shared by whoever lived in the house. Since the living room was separate, we decided to rent it out also, to a single person, but without cooking privileges. The upstairs was rented to a couple with an elderly father.

The couple worked out okay, but the young man in the living room was in trouble; he lost his job and couldn't pay his weekly rent. He promised he'd pay in a week or two. We were naive at that time and believed him. One morning, we discovered he had left through a window the night before and all he left behind was his garbage. I like to think that we learned from that experience not to be so trusting, but in the future another incident convinced me that we had not learned much.

It was a few years later, in 1955, that I was pregnant and I wanted to buy and move into a bungalow and finish the basement so that it would be suitable for renting for the much-needed help with the mortgage. We were forewarned to interview a few prospective renters and then make our choice. We rented to a couple with a young child and thought their stay would have some permanency. Soon it was evident that the woman was pregnant, and now there were two young children to contend with. I allowed them to use my washer and dryer, remembering how our first landlady had not permitted it, and I figured that as long as they were not too much trouble, everything would be fine. Within a year, their third child was born, the husband lost his job and they were not able to pay their monthly rent, although they were expecting some help from family and unemployment insurance.

We explained to them that we were relying on that rent income to cover our mortgage payments. They understood but added that you could not get blood out of a stone. We gave them notice to move, and eventually they did, without paying the back rent. We asked them to leave behind their furniture as a sign of good faith, but they told us a new story — all their furniture was rented, and the only thing that belonged to them outright was a sewing machine, a Christmas gift from some family member. They offered to leave behind the machine as a security for the rent owed, since they claimed the machine had great sentimental value. Of course, the machine is still with me. It has been more than forty years, so I doubt they're coming back for it. It serves me as a reminder not to be so gullible.

I used this old machine to do any fixing needed while the children were young, and years later many Barbie doll dresses were sewn on this old machine. At least I had pleasure in this. When I complained to my children that the machine was not working properly (because it was so old), they suggested I purchase a new one, but I refused. By then it was a symbol of our young trusting years, and how vulnerable we were to deceit.

And so life went on and we managed fine. Neither of us had a jealous nature, even though we watched some of our contemporaries getting ahead financially. After all, we had three healthy children — Sharon in 1955, Marlene in 1957 and Neal in 1960 — and the basic necessities. Soon, I was working in Rubin's insurance office when required, and while the children were young, we hired a babysitter. It was not possible to work days while the children were not in school, and we spent many evenings working.

Things did not come to us easily. I remember dreaming about having the driveway paved so the children could ride their bicycles, skip rope or play on the driveway where I could keep an eye on them. This was more important to us than having new clothes or other luxuries. Eventually, we made other improvements — we remodelled the kitchen, put up wallpaper and had the basement redone. No more renting. When we felt we could afford it, we went out with friends on Saturday nights, as we needed some time for ourselves.

Around 1970, when the children got older, we felt very cramped in the small bungalow and started looking for a bigger house. We also needed more space for the office and felt the need for an extra person to work in the office. We gathered all the savings we had and found a house in a new developing area, where the prices were not too steep. It was a big house, five bedrooms, on Sydnor Road. The children were able to pick out their own rooms; they were by then teenagers, and needed their space and privacy.

I was very excited being able to choose wallpapers and some carpeting; it was very important to me to have a nicely decorated home. It was less important to Rubin, but he liked to show off, so he went along to a point. We finished one room in the basement to serve as an office and hired a secretary. I was still working in the office some of the time, sometimes evenings. Rubin wanted me to put in more hours, which I was not willing to do. I wanted to watch a soap opera or go to the gym for exercise and swimming. He was very angry about this because soon he would have to hire another person for the office, which would mean more expenses. He was very stingy, not just with me, but also for himself. He'd have me spend hours on the phone contacting people with connections who would be able to get whatever we needed for less, whether it was something for the house or clothing for any one of us. I hated that shopping around and would rather not have the item.

As for my clothes, he'd allow me to pick out something from our friends' store, Phillips Ladies' Wear, as they usually sold it to us at wholesale prices. I didn't like their merchandise but it seemed I had little choice; it was either buy it, forget it or fight about it. I resented this very much, but I was resigned. It seems my motto at the time was "Don't rock the boat." I wanted peace at any price, and I had no stamina for standing up to him or for the verbal abuse that would follow. I got a lot of verbal abuse anyway; if something went wrong, it was usually my fault. He would yell at me for all sorts of minor things, such as a newspaper he either could not find or which had not come on time.

We all got some of his raging. Some hurts are branded into my memory. One day, I decided to go to Centerpoint Mall to do some shopping. I asked whether I should prepare his lunch before leaving but he said not to, and would I wait a while and he'd give me a lift, as he was going out on business anyway. It was taking longer than anticipated, and I informed him that I was going to take the bus, but he insisted I wait. On the short drive he was exploding about me not being patient, screaming. I wanted to get out of the car, out of that abuse, but I did not have the guts. At dinnertime, things were as usual. But it was strange that the incident was never talked over later, or ever, by either one of us. It was as if it had never happened.

One day he became furious when one of the kids said, "Come, look how Daddy filled up his cereal bowl to the rim!" He started yelling furiously, "Come, look at the animals in the zoo!" and walked out. I cannot forget his rage. Again, it was not talked about or mentioned after the rage subsided — not by me, by the children or by him. Neither of us apologized for or resolved these kinds of situations. A real dysfunctional family.

Once, when I forgot to bring a card to go with a cheque for some simcha we were attending, he gave me a look that could kill and started talking like some calamity had just taken place. I promised

I'd send the card and cheque the next day, but that did not calm him down, and we drove home with him mad and me silent but exploding inwardly, thinking, what's the use; he doesn't want to hear my explanations or apology, he just wants to be angry. The next day, everything was as usual — I felt sad and carried on while nothing was resolved or brought to a closure. How often he harped on the fact that I could not help in any business ventures. True, but he wanted to be in charge anyway. He also harped on the fact that other wives baked more, entertained more, were better hostesses. How he dwelled on the illusion that some of our friends who were much better off financially didn't spend money as easily as I wanted to, how I was such a spendthrift because I didn't work for it as hard as he did. He had a hairline temper and flew off the handle at the drop of a hat, but he could control himself if certain people who mattered to him were around. I do not cry easily, but I often cried from frustration. I felt belittled. These long-buried memories, and others, come forth when I least expect it.

I wanted to be around him as little as possible, which was very hard, since the office was in the house. I wonder how much of the tension the children sensed. I didn't run him down to them, although I sometimes let them know that I felt he was irrational. All three of them knew he had a terrible temper and they each handled it in their own way. Marlene removed herself from the home situation and went away to school, never to return for good. She adjusted to living in inferior accommodations and lived on a shoestring, but I was helpless to give her any financial support. Sharon tried to live with it, as she had no other place to go; I think she was relieved to get married. Neal learned how to grin and bear it and cooperate wherever possible.

I loved it when Rubin was out for the evening, whether on business or pleasure, or on a trip. I'd take a deep breath of relief at the peace and quiet. I was terrified of his temper. I weighed my words before talking to avoid outbursts. I talked very little, mostly just functional talk. I was walking on eggshells and sweeping hurts under the rug. I seldom expressed my feelings and said only what I felt he wanted to hear. I had no guts to stand up for myself; I didn't know I had any rights. I was a wimp, letting myself be dominated. To this day, the memories of these incidents, and so many others, prey on me. I do not feel able to erase them.

At one point, I turned to exercise and diet, as that was all I had control over. Later, it became a pleasant habit and outlet for my frustrations. Rubin said I was becoming a health nut, obsessed. He never mentioned or complimented me on my perseverance and good results. I felt so inadequate and inferior. I started searching for my own identity and realized I didn't have much of my own; it was another person's values and outlook that I had learned to accept as my own. It took me a long time to realize and accept that. Society does not allow women to refuse demands from their husband, children or employer until they fall ill. Many women are morally and economically unable to say no. I had so much anger stored up.

Why did I not get away for good? It did not enter my mind. I just wanted to get away for a while, weeks or longer, and did. Why did it not enter my consciousness even when I was away and saw how the tension lifted from my mind and body? Perhaps I was in denial and did not wish to think about it. Since my self-worth was below zero, I had no skills to think things through. All I knew was that I was stressed out and that Rubin's very presence bugged me. I just dealt with whatever was dished out and tried to avoid future encounters, sort of anticipating them, not wanting to think they would actually happen. I had no long-range or immediate plans except looking for excuses and explanations as to why I wanted to get away just for a while.

When we had bought the house in 1970 I was quite attached to it, thrilled by the new house. By 1982, I hated coming back to it. It was not a home. In 1983, Rubin had a heart attack and passed away. In 1988, I could not wait to sell the house and get out. The children must have been affected by all this turmoil. Neither Rubin nor I hugged or kissed the kids when they were not babies anymore. We didn't tell them that we loved them, and we didn't tell them they were cute or good-looking or any other things that parents usually tell their children. We assumed that taking physical care of them was sufficient, or an occasional outing or vacations taken together. We had no models from our own childhood.

Years later, I read a lot of books on verbally abusive relationships. I learned that when someone keeps telling you over and over that you are stupid, after a while you believe it. People have been shredded to pieces by verbal abuse. It's different from physical abuse — the bruises are on the inside. The weapons are different, but the results are the same. Emotional abuse wears out mind, body and spirit by words, anger, moods and insults. The books made me realize there is a name for what I endured. My experiences were validated, not something I imagined or exaggerated. I read my life's incidents in the letters of others and knew they were real. A real awakening.

I know now that I was not crazy, incompetent and stupid, as I was made to believe by so many repetitions of these words. In this kind of situation you don't have the courage to walk out because you're very damaged. As a victim, you're already damaged — you don't have the skills to love yourself, to care for yourself, to feel sexy, to make choices or to make decisions, and every incident of abuse further damages you. As a victim, you just survive; you don't feel any joy or love, you just feel pain. Women feel such paralysis when they are trapped in this kind of situation that the most common-sense thing, like walking out the door, escapes them. There had to have been tremendous damage done before that allowed us, when we are like this, to stay in these relationships. I had no guts to leave. I was too emotionally weak to carry out a plan, so leaving was not even a consideration. As I read in one book about explorers, when they get lost in a blizzard, a whiteout, and go looking for shelter, they walk in circles and eventually they freeze to death. And then, when someone finds them, they're just a couple of feet from safety.

Epilogue

I intended to carry on writing my life story but was stopped in my tracks when I tripped and fractured my wrist in September 2001. Unfortunately for me, this injury developed into a painful syndrome, R S D, short for Reflex Sympathetic Dystrophy, in which the fingers become extremely painful due to shrinkage of ligaments and tendons. I was on very strong painkillers for over a year, mostly Percocet, which relieved the pain for a few hours. I became very dependent on the medication, and at times the pain was so severe that I had thoughts of suicide. I was not able to use my arm or hand and needed hired help with simple chores like bathing. I could not get dressed for months, and food had to be prepared for me. I hated the outside help that I was forced to have. Two years later, when my arm finally healed, I felt like a newborn person. I started to have faith in life once again. My health problems continued and though I am grateful that I can still look after myself with a little outside help, sometimes I think that it would be best for me to go away for a while and not think too much about how things could be different but are not.

The following wisdoms are not my own — I read them in an article and decided to adopt them for myself. "If my children tell me I am becoming confused and that it is no longer safe for me to be alone, I will believe them and not become defensive. If I am unable to get along with my children, I will seek counselling so we can learn to manage the changes in my life together. I will get my legal affairs in order and trust the advice of professionals so there will be no problems about money or property down the road. I will not complain about feeling poorly. My children cannot fix my health and such complaints are emotionally draining for them to hear. My children are not my indentured servants. I will remember to thank them for everything they do for me and I will do loving things in return. I will avoid making my children feel guilty. Age is no excuse for insults and manipulative behaviour. For as long as I can, I will take good care of myself physically, dress well and carry myself with dignity. Nothing saddens a child more than to witness parents who give up on how they present themselves."[2]

I have also learned that grandchildren are of another generation, with their own problems and customs of their time, some of which may be hard for us, the grandparents, to swallow and adjust to, but we must in order to have something in common.

~

I'd be remiss if I did not write about my connection with the family that saved my life. My original saviours, Victor and Emilia, brother and sister, are no longer alive, but their progeny lives on. Victor's daughter, Barbara, was born after the war and knew about me only from her father's stories. Barbara is about fifty years old now and she has two grown children. Emilia's three children remembered me, though they were quite young and did not know many of the details of my story. I am in touch with only one of them — her daughter, also named Barbara. She is a widow and has children and grandchildren. I know a lot about their lives and they know about mine. We exchange

2   These words were originally written in an Ann Landers newspaper column in 2001. The full list can be found at http://www.drkenner.com/articleagingparent. html.

photos and I also periodically help them out financially. I sent them many parcels through the years, and now I send them dollars, which they much appreciate.

Their parents risked their lives for me for two and a half years, and I wonder who would do it now even for a day. I translated most of this memoir into Polish and sent it to them, and they found it fascinating. The translation was a big undertaking for me and I spent a lot of time searching for words in the dictionary, but no matter how hard it was I did not want to have regrets that I could have accomplished it and didn't. I got it done before it was too late.

Glossary

Aktion (German; pl. Aktionen) The brutal roundup of Jews for forced labour, forcible resettlement into ghettos, mass murder by shooting or deportation to death camps.

American Zone One of four zones in Germany administered by the Allied powers between 1945 and 1949. The other three zones were administered by Britain, France and the Soviet Union.

antisemitism Prejudice, discrimination, persecution and/or hatred against Jewish people, institutions, culture and symbols.

"Aryan" A nineteenth-century anthropological term originally used to refer to the Indo-European family of languages and, by extension, the peoples who spoke them. It became a synonym for people of Nordic or Germanic descent in the theories that inspired Nazi racial ideology. "Aryan" was an official classification in Nazi racial laws to denote someone of pure Germanic blood, as opposed to "non-Aryans," such as Slavs, Jews, part-Jews, Roma and Sinti, and others of supposedly inferior racial stock.

Bełżec A death camp that was established in 1942 in the Lublin district, Poland. Bełżec was the first of three death camps built specifically for the implementation of Operation Reinhard, the German code word for the Nazi plan for the mass murder of Jews in occupied Poland. Between March and December 1942, approximately 600,000 Jews were murdered in Bełżec.

Bricha (Hebrew; literally, escape) The name given to the massive, organized, clandestine migration of Jews from Eastern Europe and Displaced Persons camps to pre-state Israel following World War II. Estimates of the number of Jews helped by Bricha range from 80,000 to 250,000. Although the goal of the organization was to smuggle Jews out to pre-state Israel, some used the group and its connections to escape from Poland into DP camps in Austria and Germany.

British Mandate Palestine The area of the Middle East under British rule from 1923 to 1948, as established by the League of Nations after World War I. During that time, the United Kingdom severely restricted Jewish immigration. The Mandate area encompassed present-day Israel, Jordan, the West Bank and the Gaza Strip.

Canadian Jewish Congress (CJC) An advocacy organization and lobbying group for the Canadian Jewish community from 1919 to 2011. In 1947, the CJC convinced the Canadian government to re-issue Privy Council Order 1647 — originally adopted in 1942 to admit five hundred Jewish refugee children from Vichy France, although they never made it out — that allowed for one thousand Jewish children under the age of eighteen to be admitted to Canada. Under the auspices of the CJC, who would provide for the refugees' care, the War Orphans Project was established in April 1947 and the CJC began searching for Jewish war orphans with the help of the United Nations Relief and Rehabilitation Administration (UNRRA). Between 1947 and 1949, 1,123 young Jewish refugees came to Canada. The CJC was restructured in 2007 and its functions subsumed under the Centre for Israel and Jewish Affairs (CIJA) in 2011. *See also* United Nations Relief and Rehabilitation Administration (UNRRA).

cholent (Yiddish) A traditional Jewish slow-cooked pot stew usually eaten as the main course at the festive Shabbat lunch on Saturdays after the synagogue service and on other Jewish holidays. For Jews of Eastern-European descent, the basic ingredients of cholent are meat, potatoes, beans and barley.

Displaced Persons (DP) camps Facilities set up by the Allied authorities and the United Nations Relief and Rehabilitation Administration (UNRRA) in October 1945 to resolve the refugee crisis that arose at the end of World War II. The camps provided temporary shelter and assistance to the millions of people — not only Jews — who had been displaced from their home countries as a result of the war and helped them prepare for resettlement. *See also* United Nations Relief and Rehabilitation Administration (UNRRA).

Dror (Hebrew; freedom) A secular Zionist youth movement that originated in Russia and was founded in Poland in 1915. Still in existence, the organization merged with Habonim Union in 1982 to create Habonim Dror, a Labour Zionist youth movement.

ghetto A confined residential area for Jews. The term originated in Venice, Italy, in 1516 with a law requiring all Jews to live on a segregated, gated island known as Ghetto Nuovo. Throughout the Middle Ages in Europe, Jews were often forcibly confined to gated Jewish neighbourhoods. During the Holocaust, the Nazis forced Jews to live in crowded and unsanitary conditions in rundown districts of cities and towns. Most ghettos in Poland were enclosed by brick walls or wooden fences with barbed wire.

Hashomer Hatzair (Hebrew) The Youth Guard. A left-wing Zionist youth movement founded in Central Europe in the early twentieth century to prepare young Jews to become workers and farmers, to establish kibbutzim — collective settlements — in pre-state Israel and work the land as pioneers. It is the oldest Zionist youth movement still in existence. *See also* Dror; Mizrachi; Zionism.

Hebrew Immigrant Aid Society (HIAS) An organization founded in New York in 1881 that continues to provide aid, counsel, support and general assistance to Jewish immigrants all over the world. Since the early 1970s, HIAS has been especially active in providing assistance to Jews emigrating from the USSR.

Jewish police (in German, Ordnungsdienst; literally, Order Service) The force established by the Jewish Councils, under Nazi order, that was armed with clubs and carried out various tasks in the ghettos, such as traffic control and guarding the ghetto gates. Eventually, some policemen also participated in rounding up Jews for forced labour and transportation to the death camps and carried out the orders of the Nazis. There has been much debate and controversy surrounding the role of both the Jewish Councils and the Jewish police. Even though the Jewish police exercised considerable power within the ghetto, to the Nazis these policemen were still Jews and subject to the same fate as other Jews.

judenrein (German; literally, free or cleansed of Jews) A pejorative term used by the Nazis to describe an area from which all the Jews had been removed, *judenrein* deliberately carried connotations of cleanliness and purity, maliciously suggesting that the presence of Jews defiled a location.

Mizrachi (Hebrew; acronym of Merkaz Ruchani; in English, spiritual centre) An Orthodox nationalist Zionist movement founded in Vilna, Lithuania, in 1902. Mizrachi was founded on the belief that the Torah is central to Zionism and Jewish life. The movement's principles are encompassed in its slogan "The land of Israel for the people of Israel according to the Torah of Israel." *See also* Dror; Hashomer Hatzair; Zionism.

Organization for Rehabilitation through Training (ORT) A vocational school system founded for Jews by Jews in Russia in 1880. The name ORT derives from the acronym of the Russian organization Obshestvo Remeslenogo Zemledelcheskogo Truda, Society for Trades and Agricultural Labour.

Orthodox Judaism The set of beliefs and practices of Jews for whom the observance of Jewish law is closely connected to faith; it is characterized by strict religious observance of Jewish dietary laws, restrictions on work on the Sabbath and holidays, and a code of modesty in dress.

Pesach (Hebrew; in English, Passover) One of the major festivals of the Jewish calendar, Passover takes place over eight days in the spring. One of the main observances of the holiday is to recount the story of Exodus, the Jews' flight from slavery in Egypt, at a ritual meal called a seder. The name itself refers to the fact that God "passed over" the houses of the Jews when he set about slaying the firstborn sons of Egypt as the last of the ten plagues aimed at convincing Pharaoh to free the Jews. During the festival, Jews refrain from eating bread and leavened products and instead eat matzah (also matzos) — crisp flatbread made of plain white flour and water that is not allowed to rise before or during baking.

Shabbat (Hebrew; in English, Sabbath) The weekly day of rest beginning Friday at sunset and ending Saturday at nightfall, ushered in by the lighting of candles on Friday evening and the recitation of blessings over wine and challah (egg bread); a day of celebration as well as prayer, it is customary to eat three festive meals, attend synagogue services and refrain from doing any work or travelling.

shiva (Hebrew; literally, seven) In Judaism, the seven-day mourning period that is observed after the funeral of a close relative.

simcha (Hebrew; gladness, joy) Generally refers to a festive occasion.

shtetl (Yiddish) Small town. A small village or town with a predominantly Jewish population that existed before World War II in Central and Eastern Europe, where life revolved around Judaism and Judaic culture. In the Middle Ages, Jews were not allowed to own land, and so the shtetl developed as a refuge for Jews.

SS (abbreviation of Schutzstaffel; Defence Corps). The SS was established in 1925 as Adolf Hitler's elite corps of personal bodyguards. Under the direction of Heinrich Himmler, its membership grew from 280 in 1929 to 50,000 when the Nazis came to power in 1933, and to nearly a quarter of a million on the eve of World War II. The SS comprised the Allgemeine-SS (General SS) and the Waffen-SS (Armed, or Combat SS). The General SS dealt with policing and the enforcement of Nazi racial policies in Germany and the Nazi-occupied countries. An important unit within the SS was the Reichssicherheitshauptamt (RSHA, the Central Office of Reich Security), whose responsibility included the Gestapo (Geheime

Staatspolizei). The SS ran the concentration and death camps, with all their associated economic enterprises, and also fielded its own Waffen-SS military divisions, including some recruited from the occupied countries.

tallis (Yiddish; pl. *taleisim*) A Jewish prayer shawl, which is a four-cornered ritual garment traditionally worn by adult Jewish men during morning prayers and on the Day of Atonement (Yom Kippur). One usually wears the *tallis* over one's shoulders but some choose to place it over their heads to express awe in the presence of God.

Treaty of Non-Aggression between Germany and the USSR The treaty that was signed on August 24, 1939, and was colloquially known as the Molotov-Ribbentrop pact, after signatories Soviet foreign minister Vyacheslav Molotov and German foreign minister Joachim von Ribbentrop. The main provisions of the pact stipulated that the two countries would not go to war with each other and that they would both remain neutral if either one was attacked by a third party. One of the key components of the treaty was the division of various independent countries — including Poland — into Nazi and Soviet spheres of influence and areas of occupation. The Nazis breached the pact by launching a major offensive against the Soviet Union on June 22, 1941.

United Nations Relief and Rehabilitation Administration (UNRRA) An international relief agency created at a 44-nation conference in Washington, DC, on November 9, 1943, to provide economic assistance and basic necessities to war refugees. It was especially active in repatriating and assisting refugees in the formerly Nazi-occupied European nations immediately after World War II.

Zionism A movement promoted by the Viennese Jewish journalist Theodor Herzl, who argued in his 1896 book *Der Judenstaat* (The Jewish State) that the best way to resolve the problem of antisemitism and persecution of Jews in Europe was to create an

independent Jewish state in the historic Jewish homeland of Bibli-
cal Israel. Zionists also promoted the revival of Hebrew as a Jewish
national language. In interwar Poland, Zionism was one of many
Jewish political parties with affiliated schools and youth groups.

Photographs

Molly's mother, Sara (née Kuntsler) Weissenberg, Molly (née Melania) and her
brother, Zygmunt (Zyga). Krakow, circa 1938.

1

2

3

1 Molly, age eight. Krakow, circa 1938.
2 Molly, circa 1939.
3 Molly with friends and family on vacation in Krynica, Poland, 1938. In back, on the far right, is Molly's mother, Sara. In front, left to right: Zyga, a friend and Molly.

1 Molly with her family. From left to right (in back): Molly's aunt Karoli; her cousin
   Olga; her mother, Sara; and Molly. In front, Molly's cousin Janek (left) and her
   brother, Zyga (right). Krakow, 1939.
2 Molly (right) with her stepfather, Ignac Keller, and her mother. Krakow, 1939.

1

2

1 Molly's friend Sabina (Bineczka) Goldman (right) with her sister Mania. Dąbrowa Tarnowska, Poland, 1941.

2 Molly (left) with her cousin Ala. Dąbrowa Tarnowska, Poland, 1941.

Sabina Goldman, wearing the Star of David armband. Dąbrowa Tarnowska,
Poland, 1941.

Sabina's letter to Molly, dated September 11, 1942.

1

2

1 The farm where Molly and her cousin Helen were hidden. Victor is second from
   the left; the other people in the photo are not known. Date unknown.
2 Emilia (third from the left) on her farm. Date unknown.

Molly Applebaum, 2016.

Index

The Azrieli Foundation was established in 1989 to realize and extend the philanthropic vision of David J. Azrieli, C.M., C.Q., M.Arch. The Foundation's mission is to support a wide spectrum of initiatives in education and research. The Azrieli Foundation is an active supporter of programs in the fields of Education, the education of architects, scientific and medical research, and the arts. The Azrieli Foundation's many initiatives include: the Holocaust Survivor Memoirs Program, which collects, preserves, publishes and distributes the written memoirs of survivors in Canada; the Azrieli Institute for Educational Empowerment, an innovative program successfully working to keep at-risk youth in school; the Azrieli Fellows Program, which promotes academic excellence and leadership on the graduate level at Israeli universities; the Azrieli Music Project, which celebrates and fosters the creation of high-quality new Jewish orchestral music; and the Azrieli Neurodevelopmental Research Program, which supports advanced research on neurodevelopmental disorders, particularly Fragile X and Autism Spectrum Disorders.